MW00559457

The principal objective of Th
promote the study of comparative religion from the point
of view of the underlying harmony of the great religious
and philosophical traditions of the world. This objective is
being pursued through such means as audio-visual media,
the support and sponsorship of lecture series and conferences,
the creation of a website, collaboration with film production
companies and publishing companies as well as the Trust's
own series of publications.

PRIMORDIAL MEDITATION

·

CONTEMPLATING THE REAL

WHAT IS PRIMORDIAL MEDITATION?

It is the quickening of the intelligence from within,
from the Spirit · Just as fire returns to ether when
it has nothing more to consume, so, too, the
intelligence returns to the Spirit when it
has consumed the world and itself ·
This consuming of the world
is primordial meditation ·
Through it man be
comes spiritual
man.

Frithjof Schuon

PRIMORDIAL MEDITATION

Contemplating the Real

translated by

Gillian Harris and Angela Schwartz

THE MATHESON TRUST
For the Study of Comparative Religion

Original German title: *Urbesinnung—Das Denken des Eigentlichen*
Published by Aurum Verlag, Freiburg, 1989.
This first English edition © The Matheson Trust, 2015
English translation © Gillian Harris 2007

The Matheson Trust
PO Box 336
56 Gloucester Road
London SW7 4UB, UK

www.themathesontrust.org

ISBN: 978 1 908092 12 0

British Library Cataloguing-in-Publication Data.
A catalogue record for this book is
available from the British Library.

The publishers wish to thank
World Wisdom Books of Bloomington, Indiana,
for their co-operation in the production of this work.

Our grateful thanks to those who assisted the translators
with their valuable comments and suggestions.

Cover image: "Lahul", painting by Nicholas Roerich, 1936.
Courtesy of the Nicholas Roerich Museum, New York.

Typeset by the publishers in Baskerville 10 Pro

Contents

Introductory Note

Primordial Meditation: Contemplating the Real was originally published in German in 1935. Based upon personal notebooks compiled between the ages of 21 and 28, it is Frithjof Schuon's first formal exposition of his *Weltanschauung*.

The book will be of particular interest to those already conversant with Schuon's metaphysical principles and steeped in the spiritual climate radiating therefrom. The unprepared reader may initially find it daunting. In these early writings it is as if an immense energy were forcing a passage through a narrow channel, or a huge mass were being compressed to its utmost. The sheer scope and power of the content constantly threaten to burst the confines of the verbal receptacle.

For the purpose of understanding Schuon's metaphysics, we would now undoubtedly give priority to his later works. In them he made systematic use of the terminology of Advaita Vedanta and Sufism, as well as key concepts drawn from other traditions; these serve as familiar landmarks in a vast and often complex metaphysical landscape. This vocabulary is absent in *Primordial Meditation*. Indeed, Schuon deliberately avoided it, being at pains to emphasise that he stood entirely on his own metaphysical ground. As he wrote in a 1934 letter: "I have intentionally left aside everything purely Vedantine or taken from Guénon.[1] My reflections are far too primordial to allow of being put in the shadow of a name."

This highly significant independence is in a sense underlined by Schuon's refusal to compromise the integrity and purity of his native German by using more than an indispensable minimum of words with Latin or Greek roots, even though by the 1920s such words had long since become standard usage. Consequently, *Primordial Meditation* is profoundly imbued with the existential, symbolical character of the German language, which, as he has said,[2] "recreates" and suggests qualities rather than defining concepts.

Why translate this formidable, "un-pedagogical" work? The author himself suggests the answer in his preface, when he describes his first book as "the diary of an unfolding". *Primordial Meditation* affords us a fascinating insight into the prodigious spiritual genius of a young man whose ideas were not in any ordinary sense formed and developed over the course of his life, but issued directly and spontaneously from his very being, already complete and perfect *in potentia*, just as a seed already "contains" and prefigures a great tree. Like the great sages of the past, he "knew the water of all known and unknown oceans by knowing the nature of the water in one drop".[3]

The crystalline geometry of Guénon's writings is yet more impressively evident in the towering edifices of pure metaphysics in *Primordial Meditation*. But if Guénon's writing may be characterised as "linear" and cerebral, Schuon's is as it were "spherical" and "alchemical". Its doctrinal rigour is complemented and counterbalanced by

---

[1] Schuon's older contemporary, the French metaphysician and perennialist René Guénon (1886–1951).
[2] *Castes and Races*, chapter II.
[3] See below, First Collection.

2

passages of haunting imagery and lyricism. It powerfully engages our total intelligence, penetrating not only the thinking mind, but also the depths of the soul.

This alchemical or operative quality—bespeaking Schuon's eminent spiritual stature and exceptional mastership—is a hallmark of *Primordial Meditation*: the writing already bears the unmistakable stamp of his spiritual personality. In its content, if not in its language, *Primordial Meditation* is necessarily of one substance with his later works. The nature of Reality, Truth, Knowledge and Love; the indwelling of the Absolute in the relative and the prefiguring of the relative in the Absolute; the merciful junction between Absolute and relative incarnated by the *avataras*; the nature of man; the theophany of created things and the interiorising, redeeming power of contemplative Beauty; the divine Feminine and the preeminence of the Virgin Mother; essential prayer: all these fundamental themes, addressed by Schuon throughout his life, are woven into the rich canvas of this, his first book.

Primordial Meditation reveals Schuon's sacred vocation as vehicle of the *sophia perennis*—one situated, moreover, at a time in history that enabled him to cast his gaze back over the centuries and demonstrate, in a kind of summing up, the quintessential consonance of such great "kindred spirits" as Lao Tse, Plato, Plotinus, Shankara and Meister Eckhart. One is reminded of the Taoist "Immortals" conversing together in a sunlit grove amid mountain peaks.

We can learn much from tracing the "unfolding" in this diary of spiritual treasures; and as we do so, we marvel at the new glimpse we are given into Frithjof Schuon's greatness.

Gillian Harris
Basel, June 2007

3

Preface to the Second German Edition
(1989)

This early work, originally entitled *Guiding Themes for Primordial Meditation*, was published in 1935, that is, more than fifty years ago; now that I have written nineteen books on metaphysical subjects in French—books which, in the most thorough way, elucidate and elaborate on everything said in this youthful work—the obvious question arises, what message a new edition of that early work can bring. This may well be debatable, but it is the case that I have been asked repeatedly, by French readers as well, to make my first book accessible to a circle which has in the meantime grown much larger—more as the diary of an unfolding than as a doctrinal book of the same calibre as my later writings.

As in all early works, here, too, much is expressed too angularly or too sharply: certainly, principial Truth is incorruptible and hence changeless, but with time one becomes better acquainted with the multi-layered complexity of the Real, if one has the necessary keys at one's disposal; cosmic Reality is after all an interplay of inexorable geometry and unfathomable music. The profound nature of things is changeless; with regard to the one metaphysical Truth, this present book, too, is impersonal and timeless, despite having in places the characteristics of an early work.

This being said, I may perhaps take the liberty of adding that *Leitgedanken zur Urbesinnung* is my only book in German, apart from a very free translation I made of *De L'Unité Transcendante des Religions* myself; I adopted the French language very early on, because, through my collaboration with a periodical concerned with spiritual subjects, I quickly found a not inconsiderable readership in France. The fact that there is a value, for both spirit and soul, in the equilibrium between the Germanic and Latin natures—that is, between Germanic profundity of soul and Latin perspicacity of mind, without wanting to be restrictive or exclusive in this—is already shown by the example of a Meister Eckhart, the great master of German mysticism and Latin theology. Thus I consider myself justified in saying: it is no accident if in my life's work the German and French natures join hands.

To conclude: in an era when the neglect and destruction of the German language are the order of the day, the sense of the dignity, indeed the sacredness, of the language more than ever constitutes an essential value; and I would point out without false modesty that this concern—as it were on the periphery of the metaphysical content—forms part of the spiritual message of this book.

Frithjof Schuon

FIRST COLLECTION

written *anno* 1928–1929 in Besançon* and
anno 1930–1932 in Paris

*The French town, east of Dijon, where Frithjof Schuon was stationed
on military service in the late 1920s.

R EALITY MANIFESTS ITSELF in everything. However, Reality as such cannot manifest itself; for what is manifested must reveal itself through symbols, and since a manifestation is always distinct from its essence, only in Itself can pure Reality be pure Reality: only in Itself can It be what It is and what It signifies beyond Being. Therefore it can be said that there are two aspects of Reality: firstly the aspect which beholds Reality by means of its manifestations, thus, in the immeasurable web of the world; and secondly the essential aspect, which can however be named only as the cause of the first aspect, since in it, constituting as it does quintessential Reality as such, there is no longer any seeing or seen, knower or known; this duality signifies rather the principial departure point of the relative, fragmented aspect of Reality—the departure point which, by force of its creative duality, necessitates that fragmented aspect, so that the world arises from the interaction of an active and a passive principle; for fragmented Reality inevitably presupposes a knower and a known.

These relationships can be demonstrated using the symbolism inherent in the triangle: one vertex symbolizes pure Reality; the other two vertices, which are adjacent to one another and opposite the first, signify fragmented Reality in its double-facetedness of knower or inner, and known or outer. The world, however one considers it, or however it does or does not consider itself, can thus be described as a "self-comprehension",* whose dimensionless innermost point represents Reality as such, while what extends around this principial, purely spiritual point symbolizes fragmented Reality, thus, the world in the proper sense of the word. Whereas the dimensionless core of Reality is necessarily indivisible, the extended

*i.e., as grasping or understanding itself [Translator's note].

9

domain of Reality can, like everything that possesses spatial dimensions, be divided. Thus, around the point of pure Reality arise circles whose relativity increases as they distance themselves from their central point, without however ceasing to be symbols or reflections of this point; for otherwise they would no longer have any relationship with Reality, and nothing can have no relationship with Reality, because there can be nothing other than Reality—anything conceived of outside it would be pure nothingness.

The relation between fragmented or outer reality and pure or inner Reality is like the relation between substance and essence. If the essential transcends the substantial in the sense that the substantial is completely contained in the essential and cannot exist on its own, and if the essential on the other hand possesses all its reality beyond and independently of the substantial, then this relation, which is neither reciprocal nor reversible, is revealed even more clearly in the relation between undeterminable, infinite Reality and its fragmented reflections which all proceed from Being; Being is, in a manner of speaking— if a conceptually exact comparison is indeed permissible here—the pivot between pure Reality, which is above, outside and beyond Being, and fragmented Reality, which is below, within and on this side of Being. As active Principle, Being is God as Creator of the world; however, Being or God is what is expressed by these words only because fragmented knowledge does not go beyond this pivot; Being is as it were the veil behind which the highest Reality is hidden. The world is comparable to a stepped pyramid whose foundations symbolise the phenomenal world and whose summit signifies Being; beyond this extends infinite space, which the summit touches, whereas space as such has no relation to the summit, even though from it an inverted stepped pyramid, continuing into the Infinite, is conceivable; boundless space is to the structure as the Ultimate, the purely Divine—boundless, all-surpassing, uniquely sovereign, all-dissolving—is to the world. The summit of the pyramid, like Being in the spiritual sense, can indeed be regarded as a pivot, a focal point, as it were, where the dimensions of space converge and are gathered up—as are rays of light through a magnifying glass—in order that these extensions or rays may again become infinite below, but in accordance with an infinitude which is merely an inverse image, limited by the focal point itself, of Infinity thus transposed. Therefore, Being is the highest determination of the Infinite.

The relationship that exists between pure Reality and fragmented reality, between the essential and the substantial, also exists between Principle and manifestation; the first member of this duality is on the one hand pure spiritual transcendence and sovereignty, and on the other hand the focal point of this transcendence and sovereignty, unifying and transposing in a particular way. From this focal point realisation, manifestation and development occur, each henceforth subject to a particular determination. This double aspect of the Principial is expressed in the broadest and deepest sense by saying that Being is the primordial determination which gathers up the pure undetermined Divine and radiates it, in accordance with this determination, as world, unto the latter's effect-less boundaries.*

Now, this double-facetedness, whether within the Principial, or as Principle and manifestation, can be considered in yet another light: namely, that Reality can be understood as pure affirmation, lesser reality on the other hand

---

*"Effect-less boundaries": when a pebble is thrown into a lake it produces ripples that become progressively weaker as their distance from the centre increases. Eventually the energy will be exhausted and no more ripples produced [Tr.].

as relative affirmation. From the point of view of pure Reality, Being is the first form of negation; whereas from the point of view of fragmented reality, Being is the affirmation which connects the world with pure Infinity. Thus, from the standpoint of the world, Being is the inexhaustible nucleus of all affirmative determinations, whereas it is contained in ultimate, pure Reality merely as possibility, not as Being. Therefore the summit of the pyramid is indeed the affirmation from which the reality potentially contained in that summit unfolds; but seen from the perspective of space, the summit of the structure is a negation, because all the extensions which can be produced from the inexhaustible possibilities of space can only be negations by comparison with these possibilities; or ostensible, relative affirmations within a negation.

Thus, everything which is actualised can be considered in a double light: on the one hand insofar as it participates in pure Reality, and on the other, insofar as it negates pure Reality. A thing is real through its participation in its Principle, be it in the narrow or in the broadest, deepest and ultimate sense; it is unreal through the negation it signifies with regard to the Principial. It is real insofar as knowledge, whose object it is, is centred on Reality; unreal insofar as knowledge whose content is not pure Reality responds to fragmented reality.

*

Just as it is impossible to observe the near and the distant simultaneously, so, too, it is impossible for a being to grasp fragmented and pure Reality simultaneously: to the extent that the one acts on the intelligence, the other remains inoperative—for which reason he whose intelligence is directed predominantly towards the diverse, the phenomenal, can know correspondingly less of the unified, the essential. In other words: he who restricts himself to those modes of knowledge suited to perceiving the diverse, the apparent—namely, the senses and reason—cannot know what is knowable through the Intellect alone, it being one with the Intellect, as light is one with the eye.

That which is most distant from the eye is the sun; for even the stars are visible to the eye only by its light. And just as the sun is at the same time closest to the eye, because the eye is an image of the sun and is one with its light, so the highest principle of knowledge is furthest and nearest; and equally, by its light alone can beings perceive the diverse, the symbolical, without seeing the source of light. The stars are perceptible only because the sun has disappeared, and phenomena are perceptible only because the light which makes them visible is necessarily a diminished light, otherwise no phenomenon would be visible, only light itself. Colour corresponds to the respective substantiality, form to essence, light to the Spirit which comes from the Divine, distances to planes of reality; in order to see the essential, the real, in a phenomenon, the eye must be far from it; so that the particular, the accidental, in it does not obscure the general, namely, that which determines its nature.

Whatever knowledge enters man is also that which comes forth from him; he cannot react to anything other than the reality which satisfies his knowledge. To the extent that a man perceives earthly things, he acts; were he to perceive the earth from a great distance, no action would have any meaning for him; thus the actions of him who perceives the world from a great distance do not respond to worldly circumstances, in that his will, absorbed by divine Knowledge, is liberated from all symbols and far removed from them. Were the eye situated on the sun, it would be filled with light to such a degree that it would perceive nothing else; and so it is with knowledge, when it is filled with the Spirit and comprehends nothing other

13

than Spirit—that is, itself, in its pure Principiality. We see the sun as such only because we are distant from it, just as we can define God as such only because of our distance from Him. But if we are absorbed in the Divine we no longer know God as such, that is, in so far as He stands separate from the world and acts on it with His Will. It can be said that light enables us to see things only by means of the darkness which is still in them, since light is attenuated by the darkness. The same thing occurs on the spiritual plane, and thus we know God, too, by means of the darkness which obscures the all-encompassing Spirit without in any way touching It in Its Quintessence.

Knowledge drives inwards, Will drives outwards. Just as the breath, going in and out, sustains beings, likewise in- and out-going Knowledge is the basis of existence in fragmented reality.

But in ultimate Reality, which lies beyond essence and substance, there is no place for knowledge to go in or out, no place it could come or go.

*

When a being has realised that his existence is a mere transposition of pure Reality, and a transposition through negation and into negation at that; and that everything positive contained in him and his surroundings lives immeasurably and indivisibly, integrally, in the Divine; and that what makes a being particular is only negation, diminution, limitation; thus that the being is one with the Divine through his intrinsic wisdom, power and beauty, and consequently no longer possesses any individual existence, while on the plane of appearances he can be distinguished from the Divine only through his ignorance, weakness and contradictoriness—when a being has realised both his oneness with the Divine and his nothingness in his separation from the Divine, the deeper his know-

14

ledge of this double aspect of himself is, the less he can insist on remaining enmeshed in this existence and asserting it in its manifold reflections within knowing and willing. Every form, be it determined from within or without, be it formally limited as the seer or the seen, is the expression of an ignorance, namely, that ignorance through which something exists besides the Divine; and when this ignorance is considered in its dual aspect, it splits into two opposing poles between which its ungrounded nothingness vacillates—namely, passivity or impotence, and discord or contradictoriness, conflict, ugliness. The root of the world is ignorance; and this ignorance consists of impotence and disintegration and produces nothing but bondage and contradictoriness.

Thus it can be said: that which issues from ignorance brings about ignorance and leads to ignorance; this also means that what issues from passivity or bondage brings about passivity or bondage and falls prey to them, and what issues from contradictoriness or ambivalence brings about ambivalence and is subject to the law of ambivalence. Thus, if a being recognizes his relation to pure Reality—because in truth he cannot subsist outside ultimate Reality or pure Understanding, and thence cannot be completely separated from It either, even in appearance—he sheds himself as one sheds a garment, he draws himself back like a veil before the sun of pure Understanding, and the rays of Knowledge effective in him work in such a way that his knowing and willing, and ultimately his "I" itself, are dissolved from within, as the dew reflecting the sun is absorbed by it.

Now, the "I" is knowledge in a certain sense; for there is no doubt that it knows; but it is also ignorance in another sense; for without doubt it does not know, not just what is beyond the factual knowledge allotted to it, or beyond its capabilities or amplest potentialities, but also, in particular, what is within its own knowing; for this knowing is proper to it, belonging to it and to no other, precisely in that it is an ignorant kind of knowing. The "I", like its archetypes ascending hierarchically to Being, is a focus of that which transcends it, namely the possibilities of all higher planes of reality, unto the highest Reality; and like its archetypes and its ultimate Archetype, Being, it effects the convergence and transposition of that which transcends its limits, in order to repeat this transcending reality within its own limits as inversion and disintegration. The "I" is a centre for diminution and negation; it produces its illusory world by means of higher reality, but can also, by means of this illusory world, return to higher reality, precisely because its illusory world is none other than a reflection of higher, and thus also of the highest, Reality.

The world, the "not I", corresponds to the "I", which is the inner standpoint of the human degree of reality, as an apparently outward prolongation of this standpoint; however, neither "I" nor world is an absolute determination; the distinction between them is relative, precisely because they exist only in relation to each other; for the absolute "I", completely independent of the world—though to posit this is already a contradiction—would be Reality as such, whereas an absolute world, completely separated from the "I", would correspond to no possibility whatever. Reality alone is absolute; therefore, nothingness cannot also be absolute; this explains why nothingness does not exist except as a mere conceptual possibility, a mental inference based on relative nothingness. Thus that which is within the "I", namely the experienced world—the "I" is to the latter as essence is to substance—cannot transcend the determination inherent in the "I" and proceeding from it. Therefore, everything which lies within the "I" and is determined and differentiated by it signifies an inversion of that which cor-

16

responds archetypally to the "I" and lies beyond it, and a disintegration of what the differentiated thing merely reflects. Thus it becomes evident that human knowledge is a relative ignorance, just as the reality which corresponds to it is an unreality; that its power is an impotence, its freedom a servitude, its order a chaos; and that everything within the limits of the "I"—thus, in the world—is based upon a mere "more or less", for which reason every affirmation, insofar as it belongs to only one world, can be in accord only in a distant and comparative, but never in a real, manner with what lies beyond the "I"; for the relative in itself has no connection at all to the Absolute and can form no part of what is indivisible, yet it depends of necessity on the Absolute. The true home of affirmation cannot lie within negation; for this reason, in negation—that is, in the world—only the negative is in fact at home and continually victorious, whereas the affirmative reminds us merely in passing of a kingdom in which affirmation is at home and negation excluded. In the world, the main role of affirmation is to pave the way for negation; indeed it is only a particular aspect of negation; negation always has the last word here, though a relative but nonetheless constant affirmation must be operative in the structure of the world, in order that negation can exist there at all and negate. The world and all its events are, in one sense, affirmation constantly being eaten away by nothingness, yet invincible; and in another sense they are negation, ceaselessly replenished by Reality but never vanquished. But one can also consider this corrosive nothingness in a deeper and more legitimate sense, as the effect of the Divine, Which cannot tolerate anything else asserting itself beside It, even seemingly, and on Whose Reality apparent reality must be dashed; and the reality which replenishes but never vanquishes negation can be considered as illusion, effective within its limits, which inflates itself in vain against the Boundless.

Thus the man who has understood and deliberated upon this will indeed recognise affirmation in phenomena and events, but will not mistake these facts for primordial affirmation, as the obtuse worldly man does; he will be able to infer the purely affirmative from the relatively affirmative, but turn away from the relatively affirmative of this world, that is, from its factual aspect, in order to pierce the two-faced illusion, "I—world", through the strait gate of spiritualisation. For, recognising that the knowing and willing activity of the "I" generated the world from its ignorance, both by inversion of the Reality received from above and by Its multiplication or splintering, the spiritual man will, by virtue of that which transcends the "I" and is not of the "I" and which eludes the negating operation of the "I"—that is, by virtue of pure Knowledge—accomplish spiritually the rectification through which the inverted is returned to its true position and the multiple to Unity.

There is a kingdom at which the affirmative in this world hints, without attaining it in any way. But this kingdom is not of this world; we can only have a presentiment of it from afar, through the darkness. We recognise the affirmative in this world as the reflected splendour of the infinite and eternal Affirmation, meditate by means of the former on the latter, without confusing them. According to the Scriptures: "Blessed are they that have not seen, and yet have believed."

He who affirms this world by merely seeing and experiencing it as such, denies the Kingdom; he who denies the world, affirms the Kingdom. This spiritual denial is poverty in the Spirit, through which man becomes like a child and enters the Kingdom through the strait gate.

On the other hand the Kingdom is denied by the world, which is nothing but the prolongation and the periphery of the "I" and its wealth or spouse, so to speak; hence the Scriptural saying: "There be eunuchs, which have made themselves eunuchs for the kingdom of heaven's sake. He that is able to receive it, let him receive it."

*

Because man is neither all nor nothing, he has no sufficient *raison d'être* within himself and cannot suffice unto himself; since he is nothing but a transition, he must decide between Reality and illusion—in other words: between the divine Will and his own will.

*

Every man would be free if he knew that he is free. If every man knew that he is in a state of bliss, then every man would be in a state of bliss.

Every man would be God if he knew that he is God. May he who has ears to hear, hear!

*

There is a harmony with pure Being which proceeds from the standpoint that the world—as the sum of all worlds and always as seer and seen—participates in the Divine and therefore can indeed be called real. This is the harmony whose realisation proceeds from manifestation, from what is directly at our disposition, from the faculties of perception and their contents; the harmony which begins by taking created things and realising Unity by means of them, by penetrating their centres and thus connecting them with higher centres until they are dissolved in the highest spiritual Centre. Indeed the contemplation of the purely affirmative in things cancels out their oppositions and therewith their diversity and multiplicity—thus, it can-

19

cels out things as such; for they are differentiations only through the intervention of negation. This contemplation, starting from created things, leads beyond them, without opposing them, into primordial Affirmation, whose fragmented reflection they are; it dissolves on the one hand the opposition between the "I" and the world, on the other hand the opposition between the things contained within the world, and finally the opposition between all of this and the pure Divine. But only that which is conglomerated and solidified can be dissolved, and thus, contemplation proceeding from the affirmative entails—or presupposes— the knowledge that the becoming of the "I" amounts to a solidification and a hardening, an individualisation of an originally free spiritual state; and because this solidification, hardening and individualisation entail an inversion of the original relationships, a form-bound existence in a multiple, unstable, relative reflection had to arise from the primordial Abiding in a unique, indissoluble, absolute divine Beholding. The seer, which was not separated or differentiated from the seen, had to harden into multiple centres, as tumours are formed; and the seen, as opposed to the seer—like the exclusive, dimensionless, immutable and compelling spatial point as opposed to endless, free, immeasurable space—had, in accordance with the seer's now-disintegrated perspective, to appear to participate in this disintegration, as if in response to the solidification and multiplication necessarily associated therewith; and had to conceal its unity behind phenomena, which then brought about the disintegration of the seer. Therefore, although in the Principle, that is, in the Divine, the seer and the seen are interwoven and intermingled, and inseparably interpenetrate each other—as do inexhaustible Infinitude, symbolically referring to dimension, and unfathomable Absoluteness, referring to dimensionlessness— on the plane of manifestation this principial relationship is reversed, and the seer, diminished to a state of mere individual consciousness, is, as "I", apparently unique and absolute; the seen, on the other hand, seems multiple, unstable and contingent.

*

Every world—or every circle of reality—is real within itself; its reality is valid because of the interrelation of its component parts; hence its reality is relative and fragmented, not absolute and pure. With regard to a circle of reality, it can be said that pure Reality is its prototype; however, pure Reality cannot in Itself be a prototype, since there is nothing apart from It for which It could serve as a prototype. The transposition of pure Reality into fragmented reality is determined by the potentialities of the plane of realisation, the primordial substance, whose form-giving limitations are, as such, not directly and causally contained in pure Reality; for otherwise Reality would not be supra-worldly and sovereign, and would not transcend all circles of fragmented reality. Reality's relationships are thus one-sided and not reversible; the circles of fragmented reality are completely and in every respect symbols of higher and highest Reality, but pure Reality is not in Itself the prototype of these likenesses, except in so far as our departure point is these likenesses, or in other words, ourselves.

Every world, every circle of reality, is definable as knowledge and known, the two are inseparable; "world" means knowledge and known; if one wanted to consider each of these elements purely in itself, the distinction between them would be dissolved and they would coincide in ultimate Non-Distinction. As soon as one speaks of knowledge, the corresponding known must also inevitably be spoken of, since one face of the coin is necessarily contingent upon the other, otherwise it could not exist, any

21

more than could the perception of darkness without that of light, or the concept of the limited without that of the Limitless. This mutual dependence of "knowledge-known" is the dual aspect of the world, in which knowledge and known repeat themselves in innumerable forms, and the basic conditions of their reality are developed and manifested *ad infinitum*. The Divine can be grasped by means of each world's limitations, from which the aspect of the divine Qualities arises; these possess higher reality and power of manifestation with regard to that world, but are, as differentiations, nevertheless dissolved in the ultimate Divine; indeed the Divine stands All-Knowing and All-Powerful over the world, but without being All-Knowing and All-Powerful in Its ultimate Suchness. Thus the Divine acts even in what is most insignificant, ephemeral and accidental, with infinite Wisdom and Power, without this action signifying an opposition between agent and acted; for the Divine acts through Its Divinity alone, without addressing Itself to created things; since nothing possesses existence apart from It, and in the realm of ignorance, where things possess existence, the Divine, or pure Reality, is present only as effect, no longer in Itself. For were It present as Such, Its All-Reality would annihilate the world, as the sun extinguishes the stars. It manifests Itself everywhere, in all worlds, whereas the worlds are nothing in the face of Its pure Spirituality. Everything, the frailest and most negligible, as well as the greatest and most significant (these distinctions are quite relative and have no meaning in the face of Reality), has a relation with It; but the Divine stands in relation to nothing, because It encloses all possibilities in Its own Impossibility.*

A circle of reality, a world, is nothing but an aspect, a state of consciousness, an experience of Reality, and thus

*This could also be called "Non-Possibility" or "Beyond-Possibility" [Tr.].

four realities can be distinguished, of which the first, using the square as a symbol, corresponds to the number four and is the physical world, perceptible to the senses; the second corresponds to the number two and constitutes both the world of the soul in the narrower sense and the non-physical, supra-sensible world in the broader sense; whereas the third is equivalent to the number one and signifies pure Being. Lastly, let us speak of the number zero, which, in the numerical domain, is an image of ultimate, highest, pure Reality, of the completely undeterminable Divine, nameable only inadequately through negation. And just as from the number one a quantitative infinity is generated which is only an unfolding—fragmented, transposed and determined by unity—of the inexhaustibility contained in the number zero; and just as, from unity onwards, the infinite, the unattainable itself, stands in no comparable relationship to zero and can only symbolise its awesome void by unlimited quantity, without ever being able to fill it; and just as all existent things are no match for those which are non-existent, nor can the objects which are contained in space and develop space and actualise its possibilities, ever fill it or exhaust its possibilities; so also the worlds unfold in an inverse sense from Being, which is the first reality. And thus the worlds, with their immeasurability, cannot be weighed in the balance against the purely real, ultimate Divine, which is beyond Being. Thus, too, the supra-sensible and sensible worlds signify nothing but a transposition and inversion of the highest Non-Being, fragmented, determined and conditioned by Being. Whereas nothingness is merely a conceptual image, a phenomenon of the possibility of thinking, and, without existing in any other way, the ultimate formula of unreality—unreality which cannot stand in any equal relationship with Reality, precisely because, as a formula, it must necessarily participate in Reality, and, as nothingness, can in no way exist; so that nothingness constitutes the only thought which does not correspond to any object, and is as it were self-sufficient (although of necessity it still needs objects, in order to be able to disregard them). And likewise, as occurs in the symbolism of numbers: if the increase of multiplicity—whose possibilities and limitations are determined by unity—is to a certain degree an attempt to realise the immeasurability of, and so to speak fill up in an inverse direction, the void which lies below unity (though in terms of gradation it lies above unity), so the development of worlds beginning with Being is a blossoming of Reality, but by introversion and negation. And if on the one hand there is a sense of having the divine Ultimateness, negated by Being, arise anew, there is on the other hand an opposite sense: that of escaping from the Ultimate, which, from the standpoint of what exists, is apparently negating.

It is impossible to understand ultimate, absolute, all-surpassing Reality, or rather, the completely sovereign Unnameable, as being One in the numeric or determinative sense, as world or even as standpoint; we know of It by knowing nothing, we name It because we must limit It in order to be able to grasp It intellectually; because comprehensibility and limitation are one and the same to human reason.

Man participates in Reality in four ways: firstly through his body and the world of the senses corresponding to it; secondly through his soul, which is not oriented to the perceptible world alone, but whose dimension is something most men are not conscious of, precisely because they inhabit only the one fragment of the soul which is receptive to repercussions from the perceptible world and is thereby connected to that world; this soul encompasses all capacities for knowledge and action as such on the perceptible plane, as well as their inward point of departure: consciousness, in which are contained sentiment, imagination, memory and reason. Thirdly, man is connected through the Spirit with the Reality which corresponds to It, or rather, the Spirit distinguishes Itself completely from the two foregoing participations in Reality by actually being a presence of Reality or Being in man, by not being different from its object and actually representing the consciousness of Being in man—though this consciousness transcends man and does not belong to man as such. On the contrary, all beings are one in the Spirit, and one and the same being. Now if we say that, fourthly, man also participates in Reality insofar as pure Spirit is connected with ultimate divine Reality, this allusion to a participation—already, from the point of view of pure Spirit, only symbolically possible in a certain degree—is quite inappropriate here, and it is as if one were to say that death is a state of man. But, using the rectangle conceptually as a metaphor, we can nonetheless speak of man's fourfold participation in Reality, even if the relative falsification inherent in every representation is unavoidable.

*

In his position with regard to the Divine, as towards earthly things, man cannot avoid being influenced by his human standpoint, and transferring his reactions to components of earthly reality onto the divine level; thus, he cannot avoid applying all the repercussions of his thinking, willing and feeling, in so far as they are positive, to the Divine, as soon as he has realised that everything which elicits devotion and love here below could not even exist, were it not a reflection of the Goodness and Beauty which are contained in the Divine in infinite measure. But he who is moved by the Reality of the Divine to recognise phenomena as reflections of Its primordial Reality, will not show love or reverence towards phenomena in themselves, any more than a man would direct his feeling, willing and thinking towards the shadows of things instead of the things themselves. But on the other hand, just as the shadows, alluding to their respective causes, can elicit similar reactions as do the things themselves, similarly, phenomena elicit their respective reactions only through their dependence on the Divine; man should become so conscious of this relationship and this cause that he distinguishes phenomena according to their natures, but without these distinctions eliciting reactions in him; rather, to the extent that he contemplates them in depth, they point to the Divine, in whose Quintessence all distinct qualities are then dissolved. When man knows the Divine completely—through which he is however no longer man, since as man he cannot have this knowledge at all—then he is so much part of the Divine that he is one with the Knowledge the Divine has of Itself; and he is therefore completely one with the Divine and absorbed by It.

*

It is as if the imagination produced lacunae around consciousness, causing it to become uncertain and ambivalent, so that it vacillates, doubts and errs; through sentiment, on the other hand, consciousness becomes shackled and dammed-up, so that its freedom of decision and movement is altogether compromised or unfocused. In the first case, consciousness is no longer commensurate with the Onefold; in the second case, it is no longer able to come to grips with the manifold.

*

A being is all that befalls him.

26

*

The Spirit alone has its sole cause in Itself; for this reason, that which is foreign to It cannot be the occasion for anything.

*

To know Knowledge: to will the Will.

*

The world is a Word of God in the broader sense. The Envoy of God is a Word of God in the narrower sense. Thus, every word of man is likewise a world or an envoy of God.

The breath is the divine Principle, the consonant the primordial Essence, the vowel the primordial Substance. Or: the breath is knowledge, the consonant thought, the vowel its expression.

One hears only consonants and vowels, but scarcely the breath: this is expressed by the relationship represented in the triangle, in which only two vertices can be set out on the same line, the third being beyond both and at the same time acting in both.

*

Every movement, insofar as it is necessary, is a return to Reality; every movement, insofar as it is superfluous, is a withdrawal from Reality.

*

Intellectual power is the capacity to see the general in the particular, and the principial in the general.

*

If no created thing can be anything but a symbol of the Divine, then even less can it act other than symbolically; not merely does it have its direct principial relation to the Di-

vine, but at the same time each thing's symbolism is woven
from all the relationships and laws—correspondingly operative in every circle of reality—which determine its conditions of existence, without touching it, their symbol. But
that which can be considered as law, as determination, is,
to express it in spatial terms, a centre, and thus a manifestation of the divine Centre within given limits of reality,
whereby that centre also necessarily manifests the centres
of less limited circles of reality, continuing to the pure
Ultimate, the highest and first symbol of the primordial
Centre—the sovereign, unlimited, nameless, ungraspable.
Thus, every centre, every point, every basic condition of
even the most insignificant circle of reality, is mere reflection, within a wider circle, of a more fundamental condition expressing Reality more directly. Everything which is
in the centre of a world as archetype, like the sun in its
universe, is connected through its own principiality with a
circle situated in purer Reality; every centre point, constituting the essential reality of its domain, is situated for its
part in an environment in which its domain or world no
longer has any meaning as a multiplicity of contents but
only as an essential unit. A tree's content may express itself as many leaves and all their movements and destinies,
but in the forest it can only be considered as a unit, and in
botany not even as a unit but merely as a general expression of such; if it was, in the first instance, principle and
centre of an inexhaustible richness of forms, events and
possibilities of all kinds, it becomes in a broader sense a
mere component of a content, and within an even broader
perspective is completely cancelled out. Each thing, each
event, down to the most insignificant contingency, com-
prises a content whose principle, centre or determination
it is, and in a broader sense it is integrated as a mere de-
tail into a more encompassing content; nothing can escape
this law, for nothing is indivisible except Being, and noth-

ing can stand outside Being. Since all things are situated in Being, all things and their infinitely divisible components participate in Being; but in terms of the negating, as it were earthly, aspect of the Divine, which takes account of the world insofar as it is apparently outside the Divine, all things are merely incidental, and the Divine alone is Centre. For however one looks at the world, every phenomenon is founded upon both a centre point and an environment, and has all its possible *raisons d'être*, based on the diverse forms of expression of its existence, in these two relationships. Nothing can be manifested at all without having on the one hand a determination and a meaning through its relation with a corresponding archetype, and on the other hand, without itself determining a plane of operation. A speck of dust disappears in the face of the laws which constitute the whole truth of its existence, and all the more in the face of the Divine, in which the ultimate Reality of these laws lies; but if one does not go beyond the most immediate, outward reality of the speck of dust, and accepts its physically perceptible appearance as the only given, it is, to be sure, an incomparable fact among all other things, because in all possible worlds nothing can exist which could fulfil the necessarily unique being and destiny of this one speck of dust. No created thing can cease to be itself, falling into an existence not its own; this fact manifests the participation of all things in the Uniqueness of Being, and the Exclusivity of the highest Divine. A tree is one phenomenon, and fire, another; but the tree could not develop roots, trunk and crown from a seed in the ground—that is, it could not be a tree—did not, before it and as a prototype to it, the whole of cosmic manifestation, the core of whose nature lies in the infinite Divine, grow root, trunk and crown; and did it not, as Being, manifest supra-sensible and sensible reality. And fire, which in the physical world stands in contradiction to the tree, in that it burns it, could not radiate warmth and light—that is, it could not be fire—if the Divine did not radiate Reality and Knowledge. And the tree could not disintegrate in the heat of the fire and be burned to cinders, dissolved, reduced to a residue, absorbed, one part remaining and one part volatilised, if the divine Reality were not thus perpetually splitting and rearranging what is compounded, and if the whole world were not one day to be destroyed—burned to cinders, dissolved, reduced to a residue, resorbed.

Therefore, even the most contingent, ephemeral thing is not trivial enough to escape this web of relationships; nothing could exist without divine Reality; nothing could be differentiated, were not the divine Uniqueness obscured; nothing could arise, were not the divine Centre lost. Thus, on one hand each attribute shared by things, from the most superficial to the most profound, is a hallmark of the Oneness of the Divine, and on the other hand every difference is a sign—and at the same time a consequence—of the loss of this Oneness in the world. Every standstill is a manifestation of divine Peace, and every movement transmits nothing other than the separation of the world from the Divine, and attests to the dim yearning for the Divine and at the same time to the impotence of that which stirs, be it the inconstant flow of human thought or the aimless creeping of a worm. There is nothing fortuitous or even apparently fortuitous, since there can be nothing without a reason; therefore anything which exists in any way must manifest either the Divine as such, in the affirming mode, or the relationships of the world to the Divine, in the negating mode.

An object partakes in the Divine first of all through its material characteristics as well as the tiniest accidentalities thereof; quite simply everything that can be said of it, whether of its nature or its occurrence, alludes to a cosmic centre; has, as mentioned, a profound Cause in the Eternal; is an effect, a reverberation of ultimate motives, which for their part stand in no relation at all to their innumerable manifestations—no more than the sun is bound to anything which it calls into existence and renders visible. We have explained how everything that is manifested in any way must lie in the Divine as a principial possibility and necessity, although not in the varying manner in which the characteristics of created things are grasped one by one by the mind and traced back to their ultimate formulae. The divine Qualities are—in relation to the mind, which distinguishes them and in whose nature the justification for their existence lies—much more real than all the phenomena which the mind uses as symbolical points of departure for the understanding of the divine Qualities; while on the other hand these Qualities are as little contained and present in the Divine as their manifestations which constitute the world on the plane of fragmented reality. These two apparently contradictory truths—of which the first evidently concerns the Divine in relation to the world, while the second alludes to the Divine as absolute, sovereign, all-transcendent Principle, whose primordially real Essence annihilates all fragmented reality—find their fullest expression in the saying, "All in God, God in nothing"—which corroborates the affirming and negating modes of the Divine and amounts to saying that all phenomena are present in the Divine in a much more real way than through their individual existence; but that the Divine itself, as such and as seen by Itself, excludes all fragmented reality. The Divine is above the world insofar as one takes the world into account; but the world is not below the Divine, for considering the Divine as purely Divine and without reference to phenomena, the world does not exist at all.

This interpretation of all that exists reduces all possible phenomena to ashes and confines them to their ultimate

31

essence; for correctly focused knowledge, created things have no other meaning than this. And so too, rightly focused knowledge does not allow itself to be acted on in any other way and by anything other than the Divine, the essence of Reality. That the senses and the intelligence perceive differences in things is a consequence of belonging to the world, which estranged itself from the Divine; but the fact that pure intellect recognizes the Essence beyond the differences manifests the eternal Unity of the pure intellect with the Divine.

Every action, every thought, every movement of will is an attraction by a centre, which acts like a vortex and is a response to Reality; through death a being falls prey to the reality to which it had predominantly answered; it is subject to the attraction of such a centre, through whose mouth it must be sucked in, to be then digested and eliminated. The being falls prey to that centre by virtue of its carnal nature, its weakness, its limitation, its unreality; and is eliminated, reborn, by virtue of its participation in the Divine, its boundlessness, its reality; in other words this elimination from a non-divine centre is, in the final analysis, an attraction by the divine Centre, which manifests its dominion over all things by repeatedly wresting them from the dominion of particular centres to which they fall prey. An act, an impulse whose motivations are spiritual, is a penetration of the earthly by the spiritual, all the more so in that it has no direct meaning for the earthly. Like attracts like; therefore he whose will is not directed towards self-assertion and self-aggrandizement will meet his peers, while by the same token the self-asserting, covetous, insatiable man falls into suffering; and thus his suffering lies in his own nature, which is in contradiction to its environment, the "not-I", the world. Consequently a being, by falling prey to the centre upon which he has squandered himself in his lifetime and to which he is tied with invisible cords, falls after every death into a world which is nothing more than an exteriorisation of himself, of his own contradictoriness. Thus every man can measure himself according to the world in which he lives; be it in the narrower sense of the destinies which befall him, or in the broader sense of the whole context in which he lives, with all its furthest possibilities. The self-centred man, the believer in unreality, breaks an equilibrium which is balanced from the outside by the suffering to which he falls prey, and thus the contradictoriness of his being is broken. If this contradictoriness is not just inner destiny, but rather something which is a part of the being's very substance, the contradictoriness cannot be broken and dissolved inwardly but only inhibited and made temporarily inoperative, so that the being, if he is born into a world which is alien to this apparent, merely providential non-self-affirmation, begins to exercise its contradictoriness afresh and makes new connections to the centre of that contradictory state. For the contradictoriness of such a being operates blindly as long as he meets with no resistance or has enough power to break the resistance to which he has himself ultimately given rise; until the resistance takes his power away, overwhelms and crushes him—which again means that the contradictory being actually crushes himself.

The precepts given by the Envoys of God point to a non-contradictory attitude in man, an attitude which is in harmony with the environment, in that their most outward meaning concerns human society and the life of the individual in that society; their innermost meaning, however, far from invalidating the outward meaning, concerns man himself and the state of his spirit in the darkness of his ignorance. And while compliance with the outward precepts results from human wisdom and leads to earthly beatitude, compliance with the inner precepts comes from divine Wisdom and leads to divine Beatitude. Whoever affirms the precepts in the narrower or broader or broadest sense, affirms a general or world-encompassing order, which is the divine Will; and dissolves his own will, contradictory in itself, by becoming one with this divine Will, just as he dissolves and liberates himself—an individual determination standing in contradiction to all that differs from him—by escaping the powers which act only upon what is conglomerated, dense and solid, and not upon what is dissolved; just as cudgels, swords or lances cannot act on water, fire, air or indeed ether. But whoever denies the precepts, in the narrower, or in the broader or broadest sense, denies a general or a world-encompassing Will, the Will of the Divine, and hardens his own will through his cleavage from the world, and thus falls prey to violent, abrupt dissolution. For no contradiction can go beyond the measure of its possibility; it has to shatter against its own falsehood—just as loose earth can be broken up by hand, whereas hardened earth must be hacked apart with a pickaxe.

Men who possess science, power, beauty or any gift are but waves of an ocean, driven upwards, only to subside again. By thought and deed, man manifests his will, which nothing can withstand. His will, hallmark of his perception of reality and the belief stemming from it—his will, determined and nourished by delusion—drives him upwards until he harvests its fruits, reaches the limit of his delusion and possesses science, power or beauty or any endowment whatsoever. Nothing can resist the will thus directed, because the intelligence of the man striving for self-realisation is constantly focused on what could promote or impede his will, and it looks at everything— or overlooks it—in this light. But a state reached by such a tough, tenacious, dark urge cannot withstand its own

34

finiteness, for only pure Reality is changeless, regardless of the standpoint from which one looks at it. For this reason such a state must fulfil itself. The particular will of which it is the fruit reaches its acme in this state, becomes superfluous to itself, saturates itself in its own fulfilment, comes to nothing in its own endlessness; and if the being collapses again into the negation of his existential form—death—the specific drive of the will is dissolved, there is no longer a sufficient reason for the being to continue to fulfil this will, and remain in this illusory beatitude: illusion vanishes like a bubble and the being falls back into his nothingness, his nakedness, his gasping impotence. For his will was built on belief in the diverse, which is to say, the contradictory, and his will was a will towards what is diverse, thus contradictory, which is why the fulfilment of this will could not be situated outside the diverse, the contradictory, and could not escape the consequences inherent in it; thus the being had to fall prey to suffering, which is the final word on diversity and contradictoriness. So the wise man does not linger over the happiness or pain of his existence, but rather, judges both of these in this light: he does not drown in the seeming infinity of pleasure, only to relapse into suffering, nor does suffering restrict him; he experiences pleasure and pain symbolically, and thus he dominates any illusion: he illuminates the drive of his will spiritually, and overcomes the world—and himself—through knowledge. For he who knows the Divine alone—in phenomena and beyond phenomena—and he who wants only Reality, attaches no more meaning to the rising and falling play of waves of the phenomena around him, or to his destiny in this context, than that of a symbolism; he will abide in Knowledge through all phenomena and destinies in order to become limitless and immortal, experiencing everything in the Spirit and through the Spirit, leading everything back to the one Spirit. He will be ravished by primordial Joy, which he can no longer escape because it is real and ultimate—all fragmented joys and pleasures are but distant reflections of it, individually determined diminutions. In this sense every worldly endowment can be transposed into the Infinite, and will then signify a particular aspect of the Infinite—as indeed the least phenomenon is a particular but much less real aspect of the Infinite, and as the entire manifested world, in whatever sense one considers it, is, similarly, a particular but much less real view of the Infinite.

*

We see beings in a state of either pleasure or suffering, or in a mixed, indeterminate state; the being escapes from this complex wheelwork of states solely through knowledge of Reality. If a state of suffering has been exhausted in a being's existence, the being attains a state of joy, in which, however, insofar as he has not penetrated the symbolical experience of suffering, the indirect causes of that suffering begin to operate anew and thus lead once again to suffering. The indirect and direct causes of joy and suffering lie in each being's nature and arise from that nature, but are always due to the one ultimate cause of all suffering—namely, entanglement in fragmented reality: so long as this cause is not uprooted and removed, and this entanglement not utterly destroyed, the being remains in the domain of potential suffering—thus, in suffering. For instance, one can consider the happy man as one who has food and enjoys it, but nonetheless becomes hungry again, and no matter how often he succeeds in obtaining food, nevertheless cannot live forever and must die; thus the happy man cannot escape unhappiness except through Knowledge. However often he finds happiness again, he must still fall prey to the one principal cause of this interplay of states, and forfeit any knowledge of illusion. Before this watershed he lived in the illusion of diversity and followed his tendencies, although he possessed the freedom to perceive this illusion in some manner; but as a result of his tendencies he rejected this insight, and gave in to these tendencies despite his insight; thus he no longer has this insight after the watershed, nor as a result the freedom to follow it. Rather, the diverse things for whose sake he had rejected his knowledge of the Divine, That which leads to Reality, and demonstrated his will for illusion—these things now pursue him against his will, instead of his pursuing them according to his will, since his knowledge can no longer transcend them, and they no longer remind him of the Divine, manifesting their true, contradictory, pernicious nature, through which they are really themselves and negate the Affirming, the Real, the Divine. The being, in whatever state he may be, finds himself in constant conflict between the will toward phenomena and the will toward Reality; he wants phenomena because they participate in the Divine and because the being's deepest yearning demands the Divine, because his deepest reality lies in the Divine and is the Divine; but although fundamentally he wants the Divine, because he can only want the Divine, he nevertheless wants phenomena for their own sake and must therefore obtain them as such, that is, insofar as they lead away from the Divine. If the being previously loved them in their affirming form and because of their participation in the Divine, he must afterwards hate them in their negating form and because of their separation from the Divine, with the difference that, whereas formerly the being's knowledge encompassed phenomena and principially transcended them, this knowledge, as a possibility for encompassing and transcending things, has dwindled and now limits itself to phenomena only in their most extreme contingency—phenomena, which henceforth become reality for the being, henceforth constitute the sole, unavoidable, incontestable contents of his knowledge, and stifle his consciousness of himself; and that consequently he no longer knows that he is somehow distinct from phenomena, that they are somehow external to him; thus also that he is no longer different from them; they are indeed no longer external to him.

On the other hand, one can consider the state of happiness—in harmony with the sequence of the world's unfolding—as being anterior, primordial: whereas it must not be forgotten that in all these observations, temporal and spatial determinations have literal meaning only in the sense of the outwardly perceptible, earthly world, in the broadest and deepest sense they are to be understood as metaphors. In the beginning, beings enjoyed the world for its divinity; now they suffer the world for its unreality. All living things participate in this affirming beginning and negating end: for example Woman also, through whose youth the innocence of Paradise is manifested (which is why Man loves her); contrary to what she has manifested in her youth, that from which she is made—namely, flesh, mortality, dust—is revealed in old age. Beauty cannot remain bound to the ephemeral, because it is only completely itself in the Divine; it can be expressed in phenomena, but phenomena do not thereby cease to be phenomena or to be subject to their determination, which is different from that of Beauty. This is also evident in sexual love: in the case of Woman, the same cause which brings her to a state of pleasure is the cause of pain when it bears its fruits.

The being as such is born out of the urge to realise infinity; for this reason, everything that proceeds from the being is subject to the same urge, and everything he loves is loved for the sake of infinity; and everything he does is done in order to flow into, and be absorbed by, infinity. But true Infinity is within, not outside the being, and therefore what is outside the being can only be apparent infinity; thus all suffering is a collision with the limits of such apparent infinity, a falling back of the being into his own finiteness, from which he is incessantly trying to break out, be it on the physical plane, through pleasure; on the plane of the soul, through joy; or on the plane of the intellect, through certitude. In every joy, every pleasure, the being becomes infinite, and forgets its limits, because it does not know that what is limited can never become limitless, and that there is only one entrance into complete and ultimate Infinitude, namely that which comes from the Infinite within the being, suffuses him from within and leads back to the Infinite; not that which comes from the finite, i.e. from the being as such, and therefore—because it negates the true, all-transcending Infinite—must come to nothing, and dry up in a thousand apparent, illusory endlessnesses. Beings or things possess positive qualities to the extent and in the sense that they have lost their limits by flowing into illusory infinity—this influx signifies a participation in pure Infinity—and thus find themselves at the beginning of an existential form. Thus, in the broadest sense, that which has limited its self-affirming and self-realisatory possibilities in principle but not yet in fact, and which consequently seems to be infinite, can be called beautiful; or, a phenomenon can be called powerful because its self-affirming and operative possibilities seem boundless. That which is the fruit of boundless possibilities is beautiful; that which is the begetter of such possibilities is powerful. Negative characteristics, like positive ones, are divided into two groups, which can be called ugliness and impotence in a narrower sense, contradictoriness and ineffectuality in the broadest sense, or simply impossibility and unreality in the ultimate sense—just as one can think of the positive qualities as proceeding from All-Possibility and Reality, because the Beauty of the Divine All-Possibility, and Its Power, is Reality. Phenomena possess negative characteristics to the extent that they approach the end of their existential form, or insofar as they reach it and no longer represent the product of unlimited possibilities but rather a mere husk of exhausted possibilities; they are not boundlessly effective; rather, they appear to live out their limited power in mere self-defence. These two basic states of a cycle of self-realisation are valid not only for a phenomenon as such; within that cycle there are innumerable cycles—indeed, the tiniest fragment of every impulse is another such cycle—and these subordinate cycles are relatively independent of the main cycle; just as the main cycle of a being, if we understand by this his particular existential form—his life—is determined, not with respect to the two basic cyclic states, but at most with respect to interlocking cycles it contains, which transcend the being as such. For otherwise, no impulse whatsoever would be possible, because the being is necessarily always enmeshed in terminating cycles, and cannot participate fully in their end. Instead of considering such cycles from the standpoint of beauty–ugliness and power–impotence, one can also take the unified standpoint Knowledge–ignorance, and say the same about these as was said about beauty and power and their negations, with the difference that one then passes beyond the more diverse viewpoint of inner and outer possibilities of self-realisation.

If when considering a being—or any phenomenon—the illusion of its being infinite or acting infinitely is possible when looking at the beginning of its existential form, it nonetheless bears the seal of finiteness, for however beautiful it may be, its beauty is still limited by that beauty's *de facto* uniqueness, which is opposed to the principial Uniqueness of divine Beauty; its beauty is limited because it excludes all the other countless possibilities of beauty. And the same holds true for power, whose *de facto* reality is the inverted reflection of principial divine Reality. Likewise for existence in general, for example for mere existence in time and space.

Youth and old age—and other analogous distinctions— follow one upon the other only from the standpoint of ignorance; for from the spiritual standpoint, which transcends the temporal, youth and old age are two simultaneous aspects of one and the same phenomenon, they are two manifestations of a fabric of illusion, and their succession in time expresses only their logical conceptual connection.

The peace of men is nothing, for it is based on the belief that suffering is an accident from which one can escape. Men are strong and self-assured, because they are ignorant; but ignorance cannot be a virtue. Were they able to see, they would tremble and be faint-hearted, and that would be better. It is better to see and be weak, than to be blind and strong, for seeing may well lead to strength, but blindness only to suffering.

*

It may seem contradictory that the Divine can be comprehended as Infinity and Centre simultaneously; however the former designation applies to the Divine only as the antithesis of gravity, of the drive of the "I", of everything within manifestation that is determinable, and thus finite. Equally, the latter designation has meaning only as antithesis to the world, namely, insofar as the world is regarded as an immeasurable desert of phenomena. The centre of each and every thing is a participation in the unshakeable divine Centre, yet at the same time an apparent negation of this Centre, just as a visible object may participate in light, but is in a certain sense visible only through the negation

41

of light—for otherwise nothing would be visible but light itself, and the concept of the visible would be untenable. Thus it is with the centre of the world as manifestation, whether it is manifested in the perceptible earthly domain as gravity, in living creatures as desire or in the widest sense as form or determination in general. Everything must be centre, for nothing can be other than the Divine; the world is a fabric of illusion, repeating one and the same image in an inexhaustible multiplicity of relationships, because it can affirm nothing other than the Unique, the Real. Every thing is in some way centre, in that it is an image of the Divine, and simultaneously an incidental particularity, in that it cannot be the Divine. To confine this truth to the realm of space: every speck of dust is the centre of the universe, otherwise it could not exist. But in relation to another speck, or the earth, or the sun, insofar as these also represent the Centre, the individual entity is drowned in the insignificance of the multiple. Although in the world this monotonous multiplicity signifies distance from the Divine, as Unity and Centre signify the Divine Itself, it is for its part a revelation of the divine Infinitude, because it could not symbolise even the apparently non-divine, were it not itself a symbol of the Divine.

*

There are four causes of immersion in the Divine: the yearning for the Spirit, whatever the circumstances may be; the necessity of living from the Word of God, whether a yearning for it is present or not; the predominance of purity in a man, whether living from God's Word is necessary or not; and the Divine in Itself, whether or not purity predominates in a man.

In the first case man immerses himself in the Divine because of the yearning to do so, no matter what may oppose it; in the second case he immerses himself because he perceives that he cannot live by bread alone, that he needs the Spirit whatever his natural tendency may be; in the third case he immerses himself because the drive towards the Divine predominates in him, whatever he may think about the necessity of living from the Word of God; in the fourth case he immerses himself because his ultimate Cause is the Divine as Such, however his spirit may be constituted.

The fourth cause is the deepest cause of immersion, containing all the other causes; however the third cause no longer proceeds from reflecting upon the Divine, but from reflecting upon man, whose spiritual nature is then the effectual cause; the second cause presupposes the third—and even more the fourth—in that it is focused on man's knowledge, conditioned by his spiritual nature; the first cause is the most relative and presupposes the second; it no longer proceeds from knowledge, but only from a consequence of knowledge, and considers this consequence as the cause of immersion.

These four causes of immersion exist simultaneously in as much as the fourth includes the other three, and the first is conditioned by the other three; their justification lies in the more or less profound viewpoint for which they are respectively valid.

*

The world has a threefold root, insofar as it is considered as passive, and a twofold root, insofar as it is considered as active. In the first case the world is ignorance, impotence and contradiction: it is ignorance in that it is not recognised for what it is; impotence in its incapacity to act; contradiction as splitting. Thus the world is ignorant, impotent and split.

In the second case the world is ignorance and desire; the world, insofar as it is knowledge, is ignorance, thus, non-knowledge; insofar as it is power and unity, it is desire, thus, impotence and fragmentation. If the world is regarded as suffering, it exists through its ignorance of its own reality, an ignorance manifested as passivity and fragmentation, disintegration. If the world is regarded as action, it is error, because it can arise and exist only because of the loss of its truth; and it is desire, because with the loss of Truth, it lost Unity, Harmony, Perfection.

*

To grasp the idea that the world is only a reflection, and all it contains is nothing of what is infinite in Reality— this understanding is everything. Outside it, there is only suffering. He who does not grasp this suffers and engenders suffering.

*

Man's knowledge and will feed on the world and beget thoughts and actions; or the world feeds on man's knowledge and will. At the core of the relationship in both cases is propensity towards the world or fear of the world. For Knowledge, however, there is all or nothing in each thing, and neither propensity nor fear arises from It; for the Spirit, there is no sufficient reason for intelligence and will to feed on phenomena, nor for intelligence and will to be fed on by phenomena.

*

Man is in the Divine; but desire is incessantly distancing him from the Divine. All activity tends towards the Divine; but phenomena are continually luring man into their sphere. Thus man is in one sense a being who is perpetually running away from a proximate Reality, to throw himself into its fragmented, iridescent reflection, whose multifariousness subsists only through a negation and its resultant contradiction; and in another sense he is a being who is perpetually pursuing a distant, absent Reality, fleeing again and again from multiplicity into a unity, in order that his "I" become free from contradictions and consumed in the Infinite. But time and again he comes up against the limits of these unities, which are merely elements of multiplicity and thus for their part contradictions. He flees the Divine and yet falls into the Divine, be it but a wasteland of fragments; he hastens after the Divine and yet never finds It, except piecemeal. Thus on the one hand man loves phenomena in order to elude Reality, and on the other hand, to rescue himself in Reality. In this way he wants to extend himself in multiplicity, as one loves treasures for the sake of their variety and becomes rich through them; and he wants to be extinguished in unity, as one loves a woman for her uniqueness and becomes poor through her.

*

Reason can participate in the Divine in two ways, one constructive and one destructive—by extending itself through the Divine and articulating It, and by dissolving itself through the Divine and suppressing the non-divine.

Sentiment, too, can participate in the Divine in two ways, likewise affirming and negating: by focusing on the Divine and being absorbed, transformed and revalued by It, and by disengaging itself from the earthly, denying itself with respect to it.

Similarly, desire can participate in the Divine in two ways: firstly by relating itself to the Divine and complying with the Divine Will and thus being spiritualised, conditioned and transposed, and secondly by turning away from the world and thus denying itself.

Reason participates in Reality through meditation upon the Divine and giving form to the divine Light;

and on the other hand through Knowledge and its own dissolution. The soul participates in Reality through its impetus towards the Spirit and by turning away from appearance; this turning away also affects the soul in its links with the world. The body participates in Reality through positive resonance with the Divine on one hand, be it through ritual, or actualisation of rhythm in breath and movement, or through sacred dance; and on the other hand through denial of the body, through abstinence and mortification of the flesh.

When the Intellect began to discriminate, it became unsure, stumbled and fell; thus reason, which is nothing other than unknowing Intellect, came into being. When reason began to choose amongst diverse things, it became sentiment. Sentiment is a kind of passionate reason, for it is always based on differentiation. When sentiment began to exercise will, it became desire, for desire is sentiment that animates and inflates the will. Desire collided with phenomena and withered in them or was dashed to pieces against them. This is why man can return to the Intellect: because he is desire, sentiment, reason and intellect— this last however no longer as man. He can wrest his desire away from appearances, extricate his sentiment from desire, free his reason from sentiment. Then there is no longer sufficient ground for his reason to remain hanging in the spell of differentiation, separated from the Intellect; and it is elevated to the Intellect, just as something which could only be ether—lighter than earth, lighter than water, lighter than air, lighter than fire—would be elevated and disappear.

*

A being goes towards the things to which it is subject; that which is subject to a being, comes to him. In such a movement, one is always subordinate and the

46

other dominant; what moves, does so as if undertaking a pilgrimage, and what is stationary remains so, as if receiving homage. This holds for the smallest to the largest—for the world, which flows back ineluctably to the Divine. All movements are mere reflections of this reflux in fragmented reality. And this holds likewise for any physical movement, which always acts under the pressure of a more or less conscious, more or less limited determination.

*

There are two ways of overcoming the world, one true and one false. The true way understands the nature of the world and overcomes it beyond its boundaries; the false way understands nothing of the world and seeks to overcome it from within its boundaries. The true way seeks dry ground, out of the sea on the shore; the erroneous way seeks dry ground in the sea, by trying to empty it. The latter is worldly, conventional belief, the former spiritual, lofty certitude. But that a whole segment of humanity accepts the erroneous way of overcoming the world as the principle behind all systems of thought and all institutions, all endeavour and activity whatever—this is only possible in our era, which approaches its end ever more inexorably.

The right way is unifying, spiritual; it leads back to the inner Self and brings about harmony. The wrong way is ramifying, focused on the gross senses, driving towards the exterior, engendering contradiction. The right way masters human society in terms of what transcends it—the Eternal, which is its ultimate determination. The wrong way defrauds society with the subterfuge of its most superficial, limited well-being, as if man as such, and, moreover, in his most ephemeral aspect, the body, bore his sufficient reason in himself and could be the measure and aim of himself and all things.

At the farthest remove from the righteous man is the gratification of his clinging senses for their own sake; at the farthest remove from the unrighteous man is sacrifice—every act which does not promote the maintenance and furtherance of illusion.

Because all things which can call forth and determine movements great and small are reflections of the Divine, and only as such have the power to bring about these movements, an abandonment to these things which ignores their dependence on the pure Divine, and exists for the sake of the things themselves, is nothing but idolatry and is subject to the same law as idolatry. On the one hand symbols are good, in that they are reminders, in the sensible domain, of the supra-sensible, and he who knows how to reach the spiritual by means of the symbolic is no idolater. On the other hand, symbols, whether images or words or rituals or living creatures or foods or other phenomena, are bad insofar as they divert us from the supra-sensible and fetter us to the sensible. But in both cases it is not a question of what an aspect of the Divine expresses, good or bad, but rather, a question of the man who can or cannot make use of such expression. Thus people are not idolaters because of their symbols—they can be so only through the disposition of their minds. He who puts his faith in appearances, serves idols, but he who believes in the spiritual, or rather, has knowledge of the spiritual, serves Truth—whether or not he uses a symbol to meditate, and whatever kind of symbol it may be.

*

We want; but we must understand what we want, and that we want it.

We understand; but we must know what we understand, and that we understand it.

*

The uncertainty of our outward, earthly reality should never encroach upon the certainty of our inner, divine Reality. For the more we know that we are on one hand imperfect in the imperfect world, the more we should know that we are on the other hand perfect in perfect Reality. In this way we shall also be perfect in the world.

*

Man is in principle more than the earth; for he walks upon it with his feet. Therefore his spirit also is more than the world; for it, too, walks upon it with its feet. Jesus walked upon water and was raised up from the earth at the time of his Transfiguration; therefore the spirit, too, can walk upon the waters of the world and be raised up from the world.

*

It is said that it is selfishness to wish to free oneself from the world; but he who frees himself from the world simultaneously disburdens the world of himself. For man is only deceit, accusation and destruction; if he does not strive for his liberation, he serves the powers of bondage. Therefore none can pay the world a better service than to overcome it, at the risk of being accused of selfishness. But is there a greater selfishness than serving the world, which is woven of selfishness; and can it be selfish to escape selfishness?

*

Nothing can be attained without sacrifice; the fulfilment of the smallest act of wanting is connected with sacrifice. Even if one does not want to suffocate, one must still breathe. He who wanted everything would have to sacrifice everything.

49

*

All that man as such can do is to negate and bring about negation.

*

As soon as Reality is sufficiently grasped, the will for Reality is a decisive necessity, and not a matter of opinion or circumstances. As directly and decisively as he withdraws his hand from the fire as soon as he feels its heat, a man withdraws his will from the world as soon as he understands it.

*

A being is, from his earliest beginnings until the dissolution of his body, a party to the fate of his whole species, and ultimately to that of all creation; thus, the creation of the world was a rupture, like birth, and this is how the symbol of the *Omphalos** is to be understood. Just like the individual being, so, too, his species, in the narrower and broader sense, and finally creation, too, will die, disintegrate, pass away.

*

Appearances are false because they come from the world, and reactions to appearances are false because they come from the "I".

*

Everything a being does participates, like the being himself, in the Divine. However, this participation transcends the being, and encompasses and empowers his will without fulfilling it. When a being becomes aware of this participation he also wants, within his limits, to participate in the Divine, and to develop within his lesser

*i.e. the Navel of the World [Tr.].

reality, in each action, inward or outward, a participation which is in itself real; and to know to what extent the respective action corresponds to ultimate Principles. This is especially important in all necessary acts of everyday life, such as eating. He who does not eat reverently and with a collected mind, and does not know what he is doing, participates only in the animal aspect of eating and is merely nourishing his body, and even this to its detriment. Everything that is not done in the name of the Divine is done in the name of the unreal, the apparent, the illusory, the carnal; and it benefits a being only in a quite relative way—meaning ultimately that it does not benefit him at all.

*

Pleasure rivets consciousness and will to one sole content and makes them despise everything else; accordingly it is a symbol of pure Joy, in which consciousness and will are undivided. In the case of enjoyment, however, consciousness and will are fettered from outside by belief in an object different from them. In the case of pure Joy, on the other hand, consciousness and will fulfil their ultimate possibility and determination, because their abiding in the One and their contempt of everything which is not Essence arise automatically from the consistent perfecting, deepening and principialisation of consciousness and will. The joy which is one among many cannot lay claim to a knowing and a willing other than through its exclusivity, which does the rest of the world an injustice. Unique Joy, of which all joys are mere symbols, has its exclusivity in Itself, because It is pure exclusivity through Its nature. It is in the nature of divine Consciousness and Will to have only themselves as content; hence the longing of diminished consciousness and will for unity and exclusivity. The greatest pleasure is that which allows no other to be heard, and neither knows nor wants to know of the existence of other pleasures; but if in the case of pleasures this can occur only through ignorance, agitation and loss of self, it is knowledge, harmony and self-realisation that underlie primordial Joy. The motives for pleasure are basically unjustified, blind, violent; the motives for primordial Joy are the Self-Evident, Original and Eternal as such, they are axiomatic and require no content to justify them.

*

The narrower and wider environment in which a being is born is the fruit of his actions, that is, in the deeper sense, of himself. As a phenomenon, the being is himself his own fruit; therefore the world and the "I" are the initially given facts the being must accept as divine determination. But with respect to this determination the spirit is free, and can therefore, as an idea, cut into these facts, and plant a tree for the being, whose fruit he will be after death. The being is simultaneously not free and free, not free insofar as he is of himself; free, insofar as he is of the Divine.

*

There are two ways of dissolving the error that is the phenomenal world: firstly, the way that traces phenomena back to their divine, real Essence, and sees and experiences, by means of phenomena, nothing other than the one, non-differentiated, spiritual, pure Divine: the way of understanding oneself by means of this unifying, permeating, dissolving viewpoint, not as something individual, determined, differentiated, but likewise, initially as symbol of the Divine and ultimately as the Divine Itself, which alone is real. Secondly, there is the way of considering phenomena as such, that is, insofar as they are unreal; and, answering to pure Reality alone, neither hearing nor answering the diverse, individualised expressions of fragmen-

52

ted reality. One cannot subscribe exclusively and entirely to one of these ways of overcoming apparent reality, because each being is so made that he must reckon with his many-sided entanglement with the phenomenal world, and may not go the way of pure affirmation any more than he can go the way of pure negation. However, every being must tread one or other path according to his nature.

*

By considering things as what they signify in themselves, we know ourselves in things.

By considering things as what they signify for us, we know things in us.

What separates us from Reality is the heavy submersion in our dream, the opacity and hardening, the blind closed tumour of our "I", our world.

Reality radiated through a portal; there it became Being. Thence its ray refracted and split more and more, until all things existed.

What, then, is this extreme division, unravelling, multiplicity? It is Reality contemplating Itself through Itself, by means of a thousand shapes and through a thousand eyes.

This contemplation is nothing other than Reality. What we see and what sees, is Reality. Wherefore do beings trouble themselves, as if there were anything other than Reality?

Just as Reality went through the portal of Being and shattered, so its splinters must go back to this gateway and shatter. For if there is nothing other than Reality, and illusion can only be a privation with respect to Reality, while everything that is positive in illusion dwells infinitely more in Reality; and if illusion is neither differentiated nor distinguished in any way from Reality, except by suffering—wherefore do beings still let themselves be disquieted by illusion? Why do they waste on it their thoughts, which are but outgrowths of their ignorance when, the better those thoughts serve illusion, the more they distance beings from Reality?

When one yearns to possess something material, one is yearning for Reality, albeit unknowingly, otherwise one would not yearn to possess it.

*

Light commands silently; only darkness wins us over by persuasion.

*

One can want something little with only a small will, but everything only with all one's will.

*

Youth is belief in the imperfect, manhood is drive towards perfection.

*

Man acts for the sake of a goal; at the same time he believes in a goal in order to act.

Man loves for the sake of the good and the beautiful; at the same time he believes in the good and the beautiful in order to love.

He acts because he has lost the meaning of his existence; he sees this meaning lying around him in a thousand splinters, and gropes after them without knowing that they are the splintered meaning of his own self, which he bears within him—hidden, forgotten, lost.

He loves because he has forfeited the joy of his existence, which was God, when it still had its meaning and its joy.

He loves to play with small colourful creatures, but does not want to be overwhelmed and devoured by them.

54

He loves to drink sweet wine, but does not want to be burned by bitter poison.

But he who wants the former, wants the latter also. He who fears the latter must also fear the former. He who does not want to be crushed by a boulder must not play with pebbles.

*

Life's wisdom is to see the causes and consequences in appearances—the consequences in the causes and the causes in the consequences.

*

Every hour has its law. Every day is a house that has need of its foundation.

*

From him who throws away his attachments, falls that which binds him.

*

He who does not want to find the way to the Ultimate with much light must find it with little light.

*

He who seeks the Divine must seek his home in the place where he shatters his own will for the divine Will.

*

Willing nourishes sensations. Knowledge burns them.

*

What we would overcome for the sake of pure Reality is nearer to us than it is to itself.

*

No thing is impossible for free will. The will is free when it is empty.

No thing is hidden from free knowledge. Knowledge is free when it is empty.

Reality cannot act simultaneously and in the same respect on something on which illusion is acting.

He who does not make fragments the object of his will realises boundless Will; he who does not make fragments the object of his knowledge shall possess boundless Knowledge, for it becomes Knowledge as such, which existed eternally. Fragmented will is like water that flows over the earth and peters out; pure Will, which is the whole will, is like all-permeating, motionless ether. Fragmented knowledge is like fire that is fuelled by matter. Pure Knowledge, which is all knowledge, is again like indestructible ether.

The will is free. Knowledge is free. Otherwise there would be neither will nor knowledge. But at the same time will and knowledge are bound; otherwise neither will nor knowledge could have an object, but would be identical to divine Omnipotence and Omniscience, which have their object in themselves and are perfect in themselves.

Right knowledge and right will engender right action; infinite knowledge and infinite will are perfect Non-Being.*

Knowledge above, dream below; will above, desire below. Vanquished dream becomes knowledge; vanquished desire becomes will.

Dream and lust strive towards the uncertain, the unstable; knowledge and will strive to return to themselves.

These are the two ways to rejuvenation in the Spirit: contact with the Infinite, which is symbolically contained

* or Beyond-Being [Tr.].

in the finite; contact with the pure Infinite, which is beyond the finite husk.

Knowledge and will are formed upon that which they make their object.

*

Only he who masters the present possesses the future; for one possesses the future only when it is the present.

*

Since man lost Eden he has been searching perpetually; this is the origin of desire. He never seeks anything but Eden and never finds anything but its fragmented reflections, whose respective potentialities of joy can be realised only by excluding innumerable other potentialities of joy, and since they are only reflections and not the true Eden, lead to emptiness and limitation.

Outside Eden there is only one happiness—the will to overcome that happiness in the Spirit, and so fulfil its ultimate possibility.

*

Human joy is an upsurge; it has a beginning, a culmination and an end; it produces a reaction; it is dependent upon outward circumstances, it is reaction itself. But in the innermost core of everything mutable dwells spiritual joy—divine, pure; without beginning or end, without reaction, still as a mountain lake, eternal, sovereign, the cause of all that comes to pass. Nobody can seek or find more than this Joy; for nothing is more than it—introspective, repeating itself eternally, eyeless all-seeing, earless all-hearing, voiceless all-speaking, bodiless all-feeling, untouched by any light, any sound, any action, any feeling.

Asceticism is not a means to create Joy, but a way not to hinder it. One cannot find Joy in anything tangible, only in itself. Joy does not come to man; he comes to Joy. Joy is present: one cannot produce what is already present. Neither can one seek Joy for this or that reason, nor bind it to other conditions within the limits of human understanding. One beholds it and enters into it; he who does not enter into it is not beholding it. Just as the sun is indifferent to that on which it shines, so, too, Joy is indifferent to what is created from it.

He who has found divine Joy, the Indestructible, the Unborn, is no longer touched by anything else, for his heart lies in Being, and outside Being as such there is only lesser joy.

Joy is Grace: he who would seize it, loses it.

*

Every man is alone before God and the world. Man has only one "I", one unique "I", and this "I" is alone in the whole universe. If he has seen through this "I", then he has won his Centre, and with it, the Centre of every "I", and he is no longer alone.

*

Were there no absolute, completely sovereign Knowledge, there would be no knowledge at all, through either the mind or the senses. Were there no absolute, completely sovereign Power, there would be no power at all. The same holds for everything positive—for reality, power, goodness, beauty, joy.

Everything limited must exist beyond itself in infinite measure and in an infinite manner: for to maintain that there is no Infinite would be to aver that the finite has no sufficient reason.

58

*

Nothing moves man as beauty and innocence do; for this reason he loves woman. Nothing fills woman as spirit and strength do; for this reason she loves man.

Masculine and feminine were joined in one being, and this being contemplated itself; then it disintegrated and continued its self-contemplation, now directed outwards; and from these joyous and painful quiverings of two living parts, creatures came into existence, whose quiverings continue in ever-multiplying, ever newly-repeating, never-ending, never-liberating impotence.

Man and woman were one, and this One was immersed in its own inexhaustible ecstasy of love; its fruit was its love without beginning or end, without time or space. When this One split into man and woman, Its love and the fruit thereof broke into becoming and passing away, endless self-repetition, endless self-multiplication, endless belief and disappointment, endless lusting and endless suffering.

The spiritual human being bears within him the perfection of the Spirit and strength, and the perfection of beauty and innocence; thus within himself he closes the ring of masculine and feminine and is like the first human being, before woman was taken out of him and created.

Men are like light when it does not fall on any stars and wanders through the void; and women are like stars on which no light falls, and which remain in darkness. But the spiritual human being is like a star shining with its own light.

The outwardly-directed love of the sundered primordial being is not the same as undivided primordial love, absorbed in itself; for the latter was harmony as such, whereas sexual love is only its fragmented echo, attaining the unconstrained state of primordial love in fleeting sexual union. But because this sexual love is a love which is manifested outwardly, not a love inwardly perfected in the Spirit, and consequently subject to the law of outward manifestation, nothing but endless division can result from it—the plane of manifestation being subject to division; whereas the manifestation of primordial love lay within itself, in its immutable perfection.

Primordial love is lost only insofar as we consider it from the point of view of our loss and through the veil of our ignorance, which is imprisoned in the temporal. However, in the light of pure spirituality we possess primordial Love eternally, and return to its state, which had never changed. For only our heart distanced itself from this state and forgot it; but it remained in the depth of our being, and we remain with the depth of our being in it.

The love of a living being is manifested outwardly because he does not know that eternal love lies within him. A being loves other beings because he does not know that these other beings are only inconstant manifestations of his own inner essence, that he can love nothing but himself, and that what he loves is more real and more intimately contained within him than in the outer world, and that everything within himself is immeasurable and imperishable. A being loves outwardly in order to escape himself, and yet he can only love himself; therefore he who knows this no longer loves anything for the sake of its particularity, but rather, turning away from himself as manifested in phenomena, awakens to perfect love, in which the lover is one with the beloved, and which is closed and perfect like a ring.

*

The posture adopted in prayer attests outwardly to understanding and facilitates understanding inwardly.

*

Lukewarm faith or mediocrity consists in negotiating, bargaining with imperatives that transcend the human— in treating them, not according to their importance, but as human matters. Higher imperatives are those which negate the human, such as Abraham's sacrifice or Jesus' suffering. For the higher, the principial, does not justify itself to the subordinate, the accidental: it is justified unto itself, and goes beyond the individual, the relative, the mortal, with eyes closed but clear vision—deriving knowledge, not from factual, but from higher, principial things.

*

Injunction is based on principiality, and is for this reason just, obligatory, compelling; obedience is based on the recognition of justice, not on the understanding of what derives from justice. The spiritual man's unconditional resignation to the Divine rests upon his connection with the divine Will, not on reflecting, limited and limiting reason; for reason cannot give rise to resignation. The profane man weighs everything except his desires; the spiritual man weighs only what is subordinate to him. Formerly the spiritual was manifested only through injunction; now it has to grapple with ignorance, until the hour when it reduces ignorance and the world to ashes.

*

All things run their course, everything must be undergone, until Judgement Day, until the explosion of error swollen to the utter extreme—of inversion, anti-divinity, the actualisation of unspiritual possibilities.

Men no longer know what the Intellect is: that Intellect means knowledge of the Divine, and thus unity with the Divine. Reason, the fragmentary symbol of pure Intellect, is seen as an end in itself: one does not go beyond it. The knowledge attained through reason is incomplete even with respect to its own principle; it neither knows nor can do anything whatever in relation to that which it has made its *raison d'être* to know and accomplish, since its domain and its paths lead to endlessness, to meaninglessness.

*

Intellections cannot be clung to, as money can be buried and hoarded: if one tries to escape their consequences they rigidify into idols, they withdraw the animating Spirit from their manifested forms and become impotent, like obsolete customs.

*

One man is but little because there are many men: solely through the One and Only can he become great among men.

Some want to be superhuman because they think men are human; others want to be human because they think men are inhuman.

*

Where for some it is day, for others it is night; to that which some hear, others are deaf. Some illuminate the night with great fires, in which they are consumed before the day dawns; others content themselves with a small light, in the certitude of the coming day. According to the Scriptures: "Blessed are they that have not seen, and yet have believed."

*

The evil in the world is the hallmark of the world, it is the world itself. If there were no evil in the world, it would not be the world, it would be God.

The world is a ceaseless flux, a perpetual inconsistency, indecisiveness, contradiction; it is a web of aimless reactions.

On the path of others, each man should discover his own path. Each is alone, none can know and will on behalf of another; none can avoid his own path unless he wants to lose everything.

The soul of the fragmented creature is a hallucination; his image of the world is constricted and darkened. In man everything is broken, diminished, confused. Every one of his sentiments is a breach and an inconsistency, because he cannot prevent himself from knowing; each of his thoughts is an impotent, blind groping for reality, and his act of will is meaningless and mocks him, so long as it is his. But if this act of will is directed against his own erring, it is already no longer his own.

The spiritual man does what all men do, only he knows what he is doing. No man can do anything but what all men do; whoever imagines that he can do differently is simply deluding himself—and in fact doing the same as everyone. Most people do not know what they are doing, for they confuse symbol with reality, and therein know neither one nor the other.

All are seeking the lost Eden; no man can do otherwise. Formerly, people thought and acted—now they dream and err.

Only he who is sure attains certitude, only he who sees attains the light, only the wise man attains to Knowledge, only the powerful man attains to strength. All would be sure, seeing, wise and strong if they knew they were these things; for only the positive, the whole, is real.

Reality is the primordial miracle; whoever lay dying and saw Reality would arise as if newborn. Whoever had knowledge of Reality could destroy the universe and create it anew; but he would not do so.

*

The Divine must come over man like death, as a power that seizes possession of him; were it not so, death would take even the Divine from man.

*

Like ocean waves breaking without cease, this thought should always recur to man: that everything in the world is perfect and infinite in the Divine; that the Divine is the ultimate Cause of the world, and the Cause possesses more reality than its effect; and that the Divine is in us as long as we are in the Divine, and that therefore everything around us that we love because it is positive, is perfect and infinite in us.

Right thinking arises because Reality is mirrored in consciousness—because consciousness contains the favourable conditions that make this mirroring possible. If these conditions—favourable because of the participation of consciousness in the divine Spirit—are not present, the mirror-image of Reality is shattered, distorted and inverted in the consciousness, or it becomes murky and dark like shadow, smoke and mist. All human error arises because of a failure to grasp a basic truth—because the consciousness has become too weak to grasp what is luminous, clear, unequivocal. Men can least forgive the fact that one does not wish to be deceived as they are.

*

One acknowledges a person who is present. The Divine is All-Present, and rarely does anyone respond to Its presence. One responds rather to Its unreal reflection—namely, to the man whose greatness is only a participation in the divine Greatness.

The world is monotonous. It is one and the same, whether we drink wine out of an earthen goblet or a golden one. What the world offers us is outwardly multiple, but inwardly uniform. What the Spirit offers us may be outwardly uniform, but inwardly it is more limitless and inexhaustible than the meagre multiplicity and diversity of the world.

Every movement is simultaneously a movement towards the Centre and a flight from the Centre; every change is produced by the power of attraction of the Centre; for nothing exercises attraction without a more or less distant participation in the Centre; and at the same time every event occurs because of distance from the Centre. That which is Centre in principle, is undetermined emptiness in manifestation, and vice versa. The ultimate divine Centre is not present in manifestation; its reflection in manifestation—the "I", for instance—is not present in the Principle. He who is attracted by the Centre flees from the manifested, fragmented centre—flees from himself. He who is not attracted by the principial Centre flees from it, and wanders restlessly in manifestation from centre to centre, retaining none, retained by none, ceaselessly affected by the enchantment of the world of appearances, subjected to an aimless cycle of pleasure and suffering, birth and death: in these dualities the distinction between the primordial Centre and the fabric of fragmented illusory centres is revealed anew. The heart must in the end fall prey to one or the other: symbolically speaking it ultimately becomes either elevated and absorbed by the spiritual Sun above us, or entangled in, and smothered by, the earth beneath us.

*

A finite thing cannot exist without Infinity, any more than a speck of dust can exist without limitless space.

*

We know the world. But we know its ultimate Principle—
Principle as such—only as negation in relation to manifested plenitude. We know that we ourselves are necessary
components in the equilibrium of the world, that we have
to be what we are, that we participate as central, inward
points of departure for the world in its relativity, and that
the Absolute is in the Spirit alone.

*

Space is a manifestation, or a symbol, of the unlimited
divine domain of possibility. Movement arises from the
drive to escape spatial limitation; bodies come into being
according to the law of density in the material domain.
The unspiritual and fallen nature of physical limitation
is manifested by gravity, which prevents the body from
enjoying all the possibilities of space. The body is mass:
its mass weighs it down, binds and limits it, and causes it
pleasure and suffering; therefore all movement is yearning
and emptiness. But emptiness is a mere concept, not
a fact, for if it existed it would reduce all of space to
nothing; it would be the totality and the essence of
all the possibilities of space. All motion is impulse and
dissolving of mass, through which each thing and being
is formed around a centre, a core, like planets around
a sun. It can be said that expansion and gravity are
causally related, to the degree that the drive to exhaust
the possibilities of space, and thus overcome space, calls
for expansion; but this unfolding of spatial dimension
has as its consequence—as counterweight, so to speak—
an increase in gravity, which then also manifests the fact
that space is not divine All-Possibility, but merely one of
its symbols. Thus here, too, manifested affirmation is at
the same time conditioned and revoked by negation. Just
as manifestation as such is a mode of disintegration, and

its content is disintegrated Reality, so also space, as an image of manifestation, contains on the one hand endless multiplication and on the other hand endless division; on the one hand the urge away from the respective centre into the boundless, and with it, expansion, on the other hand attachment to the respective centre, and with it, gravity; on the one hand the joyous flowing into the boundless, on the other hand the painful compression into the limited; on the one hand the erroneous challenge to infinity, on the other hand its answer through impotence, which is inherent in the challenge and repels it as if from outside. Were space a mode of affirmation, its content would have to fill it completely, but in any case, a modality is always determining, thus negating. Since space as a particular condition of existence negates, affirmation cannot maintain itself completely therein, and is broken up in the most diverse ways.

In the realm of Reality it can be said that the Divine is located in the Centre. But in manifestation the inner is turned outwards, and the centre of the manifested world, of which space is a reflection, splits up into innumerable cores of consciousness, in whose depths the one Spirit once again leads to the divine Centre.

Reality is not to be found in the realm of space, because space produces only ambivalence and contradiction, and affirms only because, since Reality is pure Affirmation, there can be no pure negation. Everything which can be said of space also has a universal and spiritual meaning.

Similar things can be said of time, and of form, number, life.

*

That which is mutable in life cannot, as such, become one with the Immutable. That which is immutable in a being is, by virtue of this immutability, one with the

Immutable. The immutability of a being—which can be ascribed to him only for the sake of argument—is more real than his mutability, and is, in its ultimate essence, not only more real, but rather, absolutely, exclusively, real: it is more real since he derives his mutability from the Immutable and could not even be mutable without the latter. There can be no question of a being's becoming what he is not, but rather, exclusively a question of becoming conscious of what he is. This awakening occurs through the contact of consciousness with the Immutable, which principially presupposes that it is in the nature of consciousness to be oriented towards the Immutable, and indeed means a principialisation of the contents of the consciousness, a burning up of the substantial by the essential, an absorption of that which has dimension by the dimensionless point.

*

Knowledge means being touched by Reality, inward reaction to Reality. Knowledge is an awakening, a sort of nourishing and digesting process of consciousness. Neither complete ignorance nor unreality exists as such; for the Divine is Knowledge and Reality, and can only be manifested in a lesser way; it cannot be negated by a manifestation whose origin is other than divine. There can only be knowledge and reality which are more or less pure; but since they are not pure and integral, only fragmented, they cannot be compared with Knowledge and Reality as such. One can say in justification of these concepts that Reality is the content of Knowledge, and likewise, that fragmented reality is the content of fragmented knowledge.

The possibility of knowing is incontestable. It may be flawed in its apportioning and as to capability, but as such it is not subject to limits. Knowledge as spiritual principle is absolute and direct. We are nothing but fragmented knowledge: we may know more or less, in terms of quantity and inner content, but the nature of knowing remains the same. Pure, divine Knowledge, the archetype of what we call knowledge in the domain of relativity, is pure divine Reality: for pure, total Knowledge is one with its content—namely, pure, total Reality. This division into an inner and outer complementary view of Being, or of That which Is, is a mere mental formula that we can use from the standpoint of the relative and differentiated domain, by way of comparison with its archetype.

What we can express about things or objective aspects of existence is only a key to the reality of these things and modes, and to Reality in general, and can be valid only in consequence of, and within, a contradictoriness, falsity or false precondition. Ultimately there are no realities, no real things, to which thoughts and determinations can correspond—there is only the one Reality, of which all diminutions, all existential relationships, are only relative transpositions, just as thoughts are reflections of a relatively less fragmented reality. The more real, and to an even greater degree, the Real, stands through its undivided All-Sovereignty as high and far above its expression as the principial does above the particular: the latter has its whole meaning in the former, but the former stands in no relation to the latter, just as light has no relation to the objects it illuminates, or number to the objects it multiplies. Thus thought—conceptual determination—shares the same double meaning as the world and all it contains, in that, through its conceptually and existentially accurate link with a purer degree of reality, or simply with pure Reality, on the one hand, and with dimmed reality on the other hand, it is in the former sense unreal and meaningless, and in the latter sense real, meaningful and thus a key to Reality.

Knowledge as such is always more than what it knows; Reality as such always surpasses that by which it is known.

One cannot perceive simultaneously something close and something distant, with the same clarity and in the same visual field; one cannot look at the weave of a veil covering the eye, and simultaneously at the place where one is standing. One cannot simultaneously know fragmented and pure Reality, nor be filled with fragmented and pure knowledge, according to the Scriptures: "No man can serve two masters: for either he will hate the one, and love the other, or he will hold to the one and despise the other."

*

Being is like an ocean, and its waters are thus created out of Omniscience and Omnipotence, as earthly water consists of oxygen and hydrogen. The worlds and beings swim on this ocean like specks of dust. The things that constitute our existence are present for us only to the extent that we direct our attention to them and nourish them with our will, infuse them with life, let our life-blood circulate through them. The reactions triggered in us by phenomena do not belong to our innermost identity; for they exist in and through our will, which animates them and permits them to burgeon. Fundamentally we are pure will with regard to the contents of intellections, we are pure determination, reality; and this determination is more than everything that moves as content within us and outside us. Furthermore, the will of others, as inner determination and power, and as a reflection of pure Will, Omnipotence and, ultimately, Reality, is no different than what our will is to us in our own eyes. The spiritual man looks at all things as portraits and metaphors of his own self, and thus he does not attribute great value to them as something separate from the pure, unfragmented primordial Self. Rather, he

70

withdraws his will from them, because there is no sufficient reason to answer to himself with his own will. Pure Will reposes in the pure Self and does not venture beyond the knowledge it wills, of which it is an aspect. Knowledge, for its part, is more than all willing, because without knowledge, no willing would be possible.

*

God has two emanations, one that blesses and one that threatens; one that comes from his Goodness, bringing revelations and bestowing Grace, and another through which His Justice is manifested and His secrets defended. Everything that falls within the realm of dual symbolism can be related to these two emanations.

Two qualities come from God's emanations: on the one hand, wisdom and sagacity, and on the other hand, strength or courage. To the first pair correspond contemplation and immobility; to the second, action and rhythm.

Thus the emanations are distinguished from one another by their nature: the first is Goodness inwardly and Beauty outwardly; the second is Power inwardly and Strength outwardly.

It can be said of God that He is Wisdom inwardly and Science outwardly. Wisdom and Science, Goodness and Beauty, Power and Strength: the Divine manifests itself through this trinity. It produces, preserves and transforms—realises, creates and destroys.

*

He who stands in the phenomenal world with love and hatred, pleasure and suffering, must also turn to the Spirit with love and to appearances with hatred, and find his pleasure in the Spirit. He who grasps appearances in a purely spiritual manner no longer grasps them as appearances, rather, his understanding finds the Spirit

everywhere and dissolves everything into Spirit; and
nothing leads him astray.

No one can say it is absolutely wrong to approach
the Divine other than by a purely spiritual path; for if
we ourselves are wrong, how can our means readily be
correct? If it is wrong to love the Spirit, it is much more
wrong to love something other than the Spirit, or to
love something for reasons other than for the sake of the
Spirit. Therefore, may he who loves, love the Spirit even
more, and meditate upon the relation of what he loves to
the Spirit, and ground his love of phenomena spiritually,
and thus transcend the concrete, the symbolical. And if,
beyond the concrete and symbolical, he has found again
what he loved in the Spirit, and is thus alone with his love
for the Spirit, may he dissolve this love, too, in the Spirit,
and become poor in Spirit—until he is overcome by love's
archetype in ultimate Reality, which can no longer dissolve
anything, because there is no longer anything outside it,
no longer anything distinct from it, no longer anything
purer and more real.

*

In principle, idea is greater than action. In the factual
domain an action—whether or not corresponding to an
idea—has more scope, and apparently more reality than
the well-founded, determining idea.

For the individual, concord with an idea is more real
than an understood idea, at least seemingly, just as the
individual, too, is a semblance. On the other hand each
understanding of an idea is already a relative concord
with it, whereas an absolute concord would no longer be
distinct from the idea and would be none other than the
very truth of the idea.

It is more important that man bring his life into
harmony with an idea, than that his reason alone be

adequate to him, the idea remaining important only for itself, and its possible applications not being real for him.

The opposition between the idea and the domain of the individual is conceivable only from the standpoint of this domain itself—it is a mere illusion.

*

Man knows only his own knowing; but he does not know his knowledge as such, for this is Reality.

Had we not, principially in our hearts, the whole world which we know, how could we know it at all?

A mustard seed is small compared with the plant it produces, and yet we have the whole plant when we hold the mustard seed, and can destroy the plant in the seed. Thus, analogously, we are the kernel of the world plant, which we should dissolve in order to transcend our level of knowledge and its corresponding reality—the phenomenal world.

Our knowledge is our contact with Reality through our limits; just as the blind man knows the sun only when he feels its warmth, though he knows nothing of its light and its form.

Air is a symbol of Truth: it is inhaled, assimilated and exhaled. On the spiritual plane the relation is reversed: Truth comes from the Infinite into the heart, into the nostrils which inhale the air of Reality. From there it enters the brain, the lungs, which transform and digest the air of Reality, and it is breathed back into the Infinite through the heart. In the earthly domain that which vivifies comes from without; in the spiritual domain it comes from within.

*

What is eternal prayer? It came out of the divine Mouth, it went through the first man and the spiritual man; it burned in a thousand hearts; it will return to the divine Ear when the cycle of humanity is concluded.

Every meditation is a participation in eternal prayer.

*

The first doctrine shattered like the first Law. The one primordial doctrine lives on in fragments.

The doctrine shattered, the law shattered, humanity shattered, and thus the individual man shattered. He was unequivocal and became equivocal. Limited consciousness can only diminish and destroy: its creations are ultimately only debris. Only one thing is truly creative in man: the Spirit; but the Spirit is not a consequence of limited consciousness; rather, It maintains itself despite the limits, which are but darkened, fragmented Spirit.

Limited consciousness wants to know things other than the Spirit, although it has awareness of the Spirit in two ways: firstly, through the contents of consciousness coming from outside, and secondly through understanding coming from within. The first awareness leads outwards and multiplies; the second returns inwards and divides. The world as a datum, as an accepted fact, expands in the consciousness as undetermined multiplicity and forms the first, multiplying, accumulating factual cognition. The understanding that nothing is known and nothing knows but the Spirit, forms the second, the principial cognition: it comes into being through the inner instrument of knowledge—the Heart—and permeates, transforms and thus elevates the first cognition, which flows in through the senses and is mirrored in the brain.

When man experiences the Divine symbolically in boundless space, he sees himself as blind, solidified impulse limited to one point, to which he then opposes distance as luminous, far-seeing, free, limitless knowledge. Perceptions come from the outside, and in this sense,

74

man moves in space so as to escape his profane impulse: in space which is experienced and conceived as a symbol of liberating, redeeming Knowledge Itself, because from space, in contrast to blind impulse, come objects of knowledge, liberating him, releasing him from his impulse, redeeming him. But when man sees the Divine in his heart, in the Self, he looks on space as an unreal expansion of what is vain, merely auxiliary, false, unstable, ambivalent, contradictory and changeable. To this he then opposes the inward vision of his heart as unshakeable, unequivocal—as sovereign spiritual determination. Within is the one Reality, and, following it, man desists from his habitual mode of life in order to escape from the deceptive contents of space into the eternal Presence of the Self, which is experienced and conceived as a symbol of the definitive Divine Will itself, because from it, in contrast to multiplying, ever-repeating perceptions, come the unifying, completely satisfying determinations liberating man from confusing, changeable, splintered multiplicity.

*

A falling body is a reflection in space and time of the hierarchy according to which the circles of reality are ordered. To the spiritual Principle corresponds the departure point of the fall; to the physical state corresponds the impact of the falling body. Another reflection of the universal hierarchy is the world's coming into being; yet another, the cycle of humanity with its four ages, of which the last, shortest and hardest is again equivalent to the impact of the falling body.

*

When knowledge impels man to re-evaluate the contents of his consciousness in the direction of spiritual self-realisation—to destroy or dissolve them and bring them

75

back to their unfragmented archetypes—he must not continue to let himself be conditioned by those elements which actually constitute his limitation, and thus characterise consciousness as such, as opposed to its purely spiritual quintessence. Such a dissolution of consciousness is possible because its necessity arises from nothing but the intervention of the spiritual Quintessence in the limited domain of consciousness. Consciousness expressly means knowledge that is demarcated, differentiated, individual—thus determined by particular conditions, restricted and obscured. In its centre, in its eternal Present, it is connected, and one with, its Principle, just as the reflection upon objects is bound to, and one with, the light of space. And just as a reflection draws all its effect from the light, so, too, consciousness derives all its reality from the Spirit. This symbolical separate existence of consciousness unaware of itself is like an engrossment—like sleep, which renders the limbs heavy, or like a dream that holds the soul captive, or like gravity that pulls bodies downwards. The spiritual expands around consciousness like immeasurable space, and thus, too, the ascent to spirituality is like a soaring up, a dissolving of self.

*

A cognition is its own reality: it cannot go beyond this reality and its possibilities. No knowledge can attain a reality outside of its domain, and even less can it attain total Reality. This impossibility brings with it the curse of the delusion that the mere knowledge accessible to reason can suffice unto itself and encompass everything.

Reason, like every other cognitive faculty, can differentiate and unify within its limits, which are those of the relative. Otherwise, reason would have no sufficient ground and no existence. Just as it is impossible for eyes that see an abyss to draw the conclusion that it is to be avoided, or for ears that hear a speech to understand its meaning, so, too, reason, which, thanks to its gift of generalisation, knows the world as an entity, cannot grasp the ultimate essence of the world, for otherwise reason would be this very essence. However, there is no distinction between this ultimate Essence and pure Spirit, which through its oneness with Reality constitutes Truth itself.

*

The difference between knowing the earth is round and not knowing this fact, is utterly trifling in relation to what is not known and never will be known in that same factual domain, because facts are inexhaustible, and one comes not a whit closer to the inexhaustible, however far one thinks one is moving towards it. Thus, the greater factual knowledge of present-day man in relation to the lesser knowledge of earlier man is completely insignificant, let alone in relation to all the knowledge that vanished with him. What men in earlier times knew beyond their knowledge of facts permeated and unified all possible, and in principle inexhaustible, factual cognition. They knew the water of all known and unknown oceans by knowing the nature of water in one drop; whereas modern men examine the ocean of facts drop by drop and never learn what water is. In proportion to that which one can never know, or needs to know—given that only the Spirit can make sense of a fact—there is no difference between the cognition of that which is at our doorstep and that which sustains the whole earth. And by the cognition of everything on earth—assuming one could exhaust a single fact, even from the factual standpoint—man comes, not only no step closer to principial knowledge, but not even to factual knowledge. Thus those who believe in a knowledge of the world through an accumulation of facts—and in this they cannot even be consistent enough to leave commonplaces out of account—condemn themselves through their own methods to an ignorance which is never overcome and can never be overcome.

*

The doctrine of Reality explains the contradiction of existence and points the way to surmounting it.

Man desires knowledge, peace and power. He attains the first through unknowing, the second through detachment and the third through non-action. In semblance he comes to knowledge through ignorance, to peace through strife and to power through inactivity.

Just as the doctrine of space dissolves form, including its basic elements, and the doctrine of number dissects multiplicity or quantity, likewise the doctrine of Reality leads life back to its pure primordial formula and is thus a doctrine of rectification, bespeaking what is archetypal in all existence.

The spiritual man dissolves the world and returns it to the ultimate roots of its contradictoriness.

All concupiscence is suffering and struggle; all enjoyment is pleasure and peace. The spiritual man wants what all men might desire, but he wants it in the Spirit, and not in deceptive opposition to the Spirit. He wants what is desirable through and for the Spirit, not apparently outside the Spirit and as mere appearance, mere diminution of the Spirit.

The spiritual man is everything he thinks, and he thinks nothing which he is not; thus in the final analysis he makes thinking superfluous, he overcomes the necessity of thinking. Thinking is a means to the Way, not an end in itself. When thus reinterpreted and restored to its original purpose, it is the destructive ray that burns up a phenomenon as an individual entity, absorbs it unto its essence and so leads it indirectly to unfragmented Reality.

But it is also the unifying warmth that sums up and interprets phenomena as multiplicity and therefore leads them affirmatively back to the Spirit. The spiritual man does not think that to which he cannot, or would not, be united; he does not pay heed to anything meaningless. According to the Scriptures: "He that is not with me is against me."

*

The incarnation of the Word is repeated in thought, which descends from the Spirit so as to make a circuit through the poverty of human limitations and illuminate it.

*

No man is different from another, insofar as he is flesh and spirit. Only the spirit differs from the flesh, and in the spirit all are one, just as all are the same in the flesh. One man is more than another because the spirit is more than the flesh.

The spirit is mingled with the flesh as is air with water. The spirit, elevated by its Origin, separates from the flesh and returns to the Infinite, just as air, which is lighter than water, separates from water and rises as a bubble before melting into space. Just as the air bubble is determined as a single entity only because water surrounds it, the spirit, too, is only determinable individually as a being by its enclosure in the flesh.

We live from the debris of the lost Eden, we are only fragments and produce only fragments. Peoples, traditions, languages and the arts—all of these are temporal unfoldings of the one Divinity, whose spark brought primordial humanity out of Eden. Apart from this spark, humanity possessed nothing, but the spark, too, had to crumble away as it flared, like humanity itself after the Fall.

Modern man tries to rid himself of his shackles and revert to traditional ways through dance and song, which are equivalent to the walking and speaking of primordial man.

Man liberates himself through the surrender of all things to all beings. He liberates not only himself, for he does not see himself as distinct from others, but rather as their archetype or model; ultimately he liberates by surrendering himself. The root of the difference between "I" and "thou" is the "I"; for this reason he who surrenders himself realises the commandment to love his neighbour as himself, and he liberates his neighbour along with himself.

Conscience is the touchstone of behaviour. It arises from the nature of man, who is ashamed of behaviour that is below the determination of his being.

*

Only the human can come from man as such. What is limited can bring with it only limitation and destruction. Therefore man as an individual cannot give the freedom of the Spirit; nor any kind of real good, for there is no real good except freedom through the Spirit. This demonstrates the futility of the opinion that man should be mindful of the welfare of his neighbour in the highest things even more than in earthly things. Freedom in the Spirit cancels out the difference between "I" and "thou", and no good can be done which would be remotely comparable to the good of this freedom. Nothing is better than the accessibility and presence of one who is spiritually free; nothing better can happen to any being than to meet with a spiritual man. Before acting, one must be. Thus all human activity can have meaning only in relation to spiritual liberation and not merely with regard to love of one's neighbour. No earthly good is in itself a real good, and spiritual benefits can issue only from him who is able to give them. Ordinary human virtue produces only limitation; it is necessarily self-seeking insofar as it is concerned with its own welfare in another, and thus extends its own earthly needs to the generality, whereas spiritual liberation does not proceed from any social standpoint, and to the extent that it takes into account the question of welfare, it brings it into relation with the "I" as such, and not with some particular, merely factual, "I"; but the symbol of the "I" as such is perforce the respective "I" of each man.

He who, despite the accusation of selfishness, has overcome his "I" through his liberation, he alone, not only in principle by means of his own liberation, but also in fact, can take upon himself a part of the evil to which the world is generally condemned; whereas the man who is not free can bear scarcely more than his own burden, despite his claim to selflessness. Thus in the final analysis the only good that has meaning is the one man undertakes for the liberation of the world, which he must necessarily realise in himself—the good whose meaning lies in overcoming the illusory barriers between "I" and "thou" and experiencing the "I" in every man, and every man in the "I". Any good as an end in itself is a vain, foolish, presumptuous aberration, which follows from the fact that people give themselves credit for their paltry virtues, as if these were not quite meaningless and void in the face of the Spirit—the pure, unfragmented Divine, which radiates light and salvation. Apart from the Divine there is no good, since the fact that a man does nothing bad, is not good, but merely reasonable.

The spiritual man is reborn annually, daily, hourly, indeed in every vibration of his life, since, bound to the eternally young Spirit in an imperturbable present, he does not drag behind him any pernicious entanglement which would poison every new awakening to Knowledge with old errors. He is an exclusively knowing and willing

81

being who grasps the world directly in the Spirit, not as an accumulation of facts. One can say that he is not bound to himself as a past and future fact, because he is situated in the omnipresent, ever-actual divine Principle.

Just as light dazzles the eyes and prevents them from seeing what it makes visible, so the Spirit dazzles the intelligence and prevents it from doubting what It makes comprehensible.

*

That which is true, cannot be truer than true. Therefore, Truth suffices unto itself and has no need of any external reference point. He who knows the Truth has certitude simultaneously; even if he is ignorant of countless other assertions, these, if they are not untrue, can only be less true, or at most equally true, but not more true, than the one known Truth in which all possible truths are contained. Therefore the doctrine of Reality is true in the same way that the point is dimensionless; and thus it contains all possibilities of knowledge in itself, just as the point contains all spatial possibilities in itself and cannot be more dimensionless than dimensionless.

At the same time, a statement is true only conditionally, namely in the domain of a particular standpoint, and it must therefore be necessarily limited in relation to its whole essence. Thus, a statement, even if true in itself, is nevertheless relatively untrue because of its necessary limitation and exclusiveness. With regard to the unlimited truth of its ultimate content, which it partly veils and partly manifests, its specifically expressed truth can only be a relative, diminished one, just as each concept is of lesser truth, because, being a concept, it can never completely correspond to its object, while still being thoroughly necessary and as true as possible in the domain of its manifestation. A triangle cannot be more triangular than triangular, but it limits by its particular form the pure idea of three-ness, which can be expressed by innumerable other symbols, and which infinitely transcends each of them, so that although each symbol as such is completely true, only the primordial Idea possesses its own infinite Truth.

*

We have only one possession—Knowledge, and this does not come from us.

*

There are two kinds of stupidity: one is curable, for it is intolerable; the other is incurable, for one is proud of it and seeks to spread it. Most people think too much and reflect too little.

*

No purification purifies like the knowledge of purity.

*

The contradiction of existence lies in the fact that it appears to be the boundary of the Boundless.

*

Enjoyment is an emanation of pleasure; the latter is broader and deeper than all enjoyment. Pleasure is an emanation of joy; the latter is broader and deeper than all pleasure. Joy is an emanation of life; the latter is broader and deeper than all joy. Life is an emanation of existence; the latter is broader and deeper than all life. Existence is the emanation of Being; the latter is broader and deeper than all existence. Being is the emanation of the Ultimate, Infinite, All-Real, All-Broad and All-Deep.

*

The Divine is present in the heart where Knowledge and Love are in harmony.

*

You want the perfect man? Of what significance is man? Everything depends on the self-realisation of the Divine.

SECOND COLLECTION

Written *anno* 1932 in the Monastery of Notre Dame de
Scourmont, Forges-lez-Chimay*

> *Aliquid est in anima, quod est increatum*
> *et increabile; si tota anima esset talis, esset*
> *increata et increabilis, et hoc est intellectus.*
>
> There is something in the soul that is
> uncreated and uncreatable; if the whole
> soul were such, it would be uncreated and
> uncreatable, and this is the Intellect.
>
> Meister Eckhart

*The Trappist monastery in Belgium into which Frithjof Schuon's
brother had been received.

THERE CAN BE ONLY ONE absolutely infallible touch-stone of Truth: Knowledge, which no external evidence can resist. For this reason the external justification as such of a doctrine is inadequate and cannot even exist without invoking a Master who has infallible and direct knowledge.

There are two sources of doctrinal authority: Tradition, or harmony with Tradition, and Knowledge, or harmony with Knowledge.

*

Knowledge is an equilibrium, and every perception or understanding is a breach of this equilibrium, whatever the scope of the perception or understanding as such. The Knowledge inherent in the Spirit—Knowledge as such—is neither perceiving nor perceived, for it is not substantial: rather, it is purely essential.

*

When knowledge is penetrated by the rays of true Knowledge and dissolved in it, all further knowledge of which the human spirit has need comes of itself, without the mind searching for it. Therefore mere factual learning must be restricted. For the thirst for learning comes, not from Knowledge, but from passion. He who wants to know, will know; but he who wants merely to increase his learning remains ignorant. Learning restricted for the sake of pure Knowledge attracts other learning, like a vortex. No learning necessary for the human spirit is lost by such a restriction. All new learning is fruitless and harmful before the old learning has penetrated man deeply and become dissolved in his knowledge of the world; and all learning which has no sufficient reason with regard to Knowledge is an impediment. He who cannot tread the path of conscious ignorance never reaches the highest learning. The thirst for facts is the betrayal of Knowledge; through such betrayal the intelligence becomes like an impotent glance at amassed jewels. The spiritual man knows little, or rather, he knows that he knows little; but he knows this little so well that through knowing a little he knows everything. He does not waver between two words; rather, he believes in one. If one piece of learning falls on good ground, the tree of pure Knowledge grows from it. If a thousand kinds of learning fall on poor ground, a thousand kinds of feeble weeds proliferate impotently towards the space of unlimited knowledge.

*

The ordinary man allows his base instinct to speak through his thinking; he is besotted by the enunciation of his thinking and does not ask whence it comes.

The heart of the spiritual man does not lie in the instinctive, nor does he put his trust unconditionally in his thoughts; rather, uncorrupted Knowledge is his guiding power, and the Ungraspable his sufficient reason. He does not incessantly fall prey to thoughts that rise like bubbles out of the quagmire of ignorance, and justify these contrary to his own knowledge.

*

He who understands that the Spirit is free and that It alone is free, cannot consider as free that which is not of the Spirit. Thus the spiritual man leads the life of a prisoner: for he knows of his spirit's freedom and wants to be free only in the Spirit and as Spirit; that is, he wants to be truly free, not just seemingly free. Those who are outwardly and seemingly free, who live from day to day, arbitrarily and haphazardly, not guided by any understanding, are no less imprisoned than those who voluntarily bind themselves, only they do not know it, and see in imprisonment in the Spirit mere negation, instead of understanding that this holy imprisonment negates only negation, and that fools' freedom affirms nothing but negation. All men are at once bound and free: but in different ways.

*

Truth is the mirror of Reality.
Wisdom effects power.
Will answers Knowledge.
Action answers perception.

*

Power manifests nothing but the expansion of knowledge— in the highest and ultimate sense Reality—which is the manifestation of divine Knowledge. Just as one must re-cognize power in order to possess it, so one must want knowledge in order to perfect it. Knowledge is the essen-tial core of power, Truth in the highest and ultimate sense, which is the Centre of the divine Omnipotence.
Desires destroy Knowledge.
Errors destroy power.

*

The ultimate intention of every expansion is a growing into the Infinite, in order to fill It and become identical with It. Every expanded thing is doubly limited, by form and within form. Form is as it were the error of the impulse to expand. And the impulse stops at this error, for the error contradicts it, limits it outwardly, just as impulse limits itself inwardly, and prevents it from becoming pure expansion. Error is thus the hallmark and the expression of the fact that the particular, the limited, can as such never become undetermined and limitless. Within form an expanded thing suffers the consequence of its

89

expansion in fragmented reality, in manifestation; for like the plane of expansion, whose possibilities are developed and realised by the impulse according to its inherent intention, so, too, the thing thus expanded participates in the fragmentariness of its existential substance. For this reason every expanded thing is not only limited, but also imperfect within its expansion; for expansion in fragmented reality—manifestation—cannot be perfect like its archetype in pure Reality, an archetype that is not expanded, but infinite. This inherent imperfection of an expanded thing manifests itself in living beings by contradiction. In man this inner conflict extends into the reasoning faculty, where it discloses itself as doubt. The spiritual man does not build his house on the earth, which must be broken down because it is composite, not of a piece: rather, he himself dissolves that which is compound, and builds his house upon the Integral, Unexpanded, Indivisible. Every expanded thing can be measured, thus divided: it is a "more" and can thus be a "less". But Infinitude is immeasurable and indivisible, for it does not arise out of a "less" and cannot become a "less". It has nothing beside which it could be a "more": it is simply and unconditionally everything in terms of human language, but not in Itself, for even "everything" is still a comparison.

*

Nothing moves a man like beauty and innocence; for this reason he loves woman. Beauty and innocence are two aspects—outward and inward—of the same principle, so that one can in a manner of speaking call beauty outward innocence, and innocence inward beauty. Innocence is unequivocalness; freedom from uneven motivations; the essence of undoubting vitality. Innocence does not sunder, it unifies; it does not doubt, and as such harbours no contradictions. For this reason it is manifested as beauty,

90

for beauty is the consequence of such unity and cannot be the consequence of a sundering, a motivation, a doubt, a contradictoriness.

The Mother of Jesus possessed this two-faceted harmony in exalted perfection, for the Redeemer needed this heredity. It came from the first woman and was handed down to Mary—encapsulated, as it were, and having only partially bloomed in other women—and was revealed again in her as in the primordial woman. An inheritance is, however, never a totality, but only a part, the feminine part of a totality; the masculine part comes from neither father nor mother, but out of each individual himself; so that Mary's innocence and beauty, as the component we call feminine, were the legacy of something intact and paradisal, but as the component we call masculine, they were her own participation in the Divine. For no participation in the Divine—neither beauty, nor power, nor wisdom—can be made manifest without a double provenance: namely, inheritance and fecundation by the respective divine Cause itself. The feminine inheritance produces as it were the substance, the form, the body; and the direct masculine fecundation—which so to speak consummates the symbolically horizontal inheritance vertically—produces the essence, the spirit, of the respective participation in the Divine that is being manifested. In this sense each being is an heir of created beings and an heir of the Divine. It is the same with every thing, with every idea; for everything is on the one hand connected to other things and on the other hand separated from them. No phenomenon is the only one of its kind, yet each is unique in its own way.

Man loves woman for her beauty: beauty, which stands sovereign and free vis-à-vis form, is made manifest less by virtue of the formal than despite formal limitation. For form cannot be the cause of beauty, since it is not the specific outward appearance but the inner coherence that constitutes the true nature of beauty—the concordance of imperceptible causes, which arise in a thousand threads from archetypal spiritual Beauty, principial Femininity or the feminine aspect of the Divine. Pure Beauty, pure Innocence, pure Harmony are at the centre of all that testifies piecemeal to the Divine in fragmented reality. Since harmony is manifested in the fragmented, in forms, without thereby becoming limited, it cannot dwell in them; for this reason, harmony or beauty of forms is relative and ephemeral like the forms themselves. A beautiful form is the limitless given expression through the limited. The being who suffers from his limitations and seeks the limitless for his liberation, clings to forms and phenomena through which the limitless passes and in which it temporarily produces beauty, just as a sunbeam glides over an object and fleetingly makes it luminous. And thus the being never reaches the limitless, for he loves the limitless in phenomena and loses himself in phenomena, and forgets his own inner limitlessness. Man seeks the limitless in woman, and because he mistakes the phenomenon for its eternal Cause, because of this fundamental error, he propagates himself, he is continually reborn in his progeny, he perpetually repeats himself.

Beyond forms, beauty is joy—not the joy of the soul, differentiated from sadness, but the archetype of the soul's joy, the joy of the world soul, which has no opposite. If one can call beauty outward innocence, likewise, the interpretation as joy of form applies to it, and to joy, the interpretation as inward beauty: for joy, like innocence and beauty, is without contradiction.

He who sees through and vanquishes all the forms that constitute his conditioned, limited nature, and thus strives for the Infinite, becomes submerged in the Infinite, just as a spark flies into space and drowns and is extinguished in space.

*

How does principial Knowledge, how does principial Power manifest itself as effective knowledge, effective power? What separates ignorance from knowledge, impotence from power? This translation of the Infinite into the finite is expressed in two ways, one amalgamating and one dispersing. In the one case ignorance and impotence tend towards contraction, exclusivity, particularity, as a means of expression; in the other, they tend towards disintegration, division, diversity. The perceptions and modes of the will thus arise as specific individual facts, and hence at the same time as consequences, in their diversity and multiplicity, of ignorance and impotence.

In one sense man, like all things, is an illusion in relation to reality because of his limitation, his poverty, his uniqueness; and in another sense he is an illusion through his expansion, his wealth, his multiplicity. In one sense Reality consists in its Uniqueness and Absoluteness; in another sense in its Totality and Infinitude. Where manifestation is hardened into singularity, particularity, it mirrors principial Uniqueness, but contradicts Totality and Infinitude; where manifestation is unravelled into multiplicity and diversity, it mirrors Totality and Infinitude, but contradicts principial Uniqueness and Categoricalness. Manifestation partakes in the Principial and would not be at liberty not to partake in it. On the other hand, however, it stands in apparent contradiction to the Principial, and for this reason suffers from limitations and divisions and, depending on the way it contradicts the Principial, becomes riveted, captive, hardened; or rent, dissipated, dissolved.

93

*

Two things in space are symbolically analogous to Infinitude: the unexpanded, inwardly endless centre, and
spherically expanded, outwardly endless distance.

Two things in time are symbolically analogous to Eternity: the unexpanded, inwardly endless present moment,
and duration expanded into past and future.

Space has three dimensions, because it corresponds to
the conserving, extending, affirming principle, manifested
by triplicity, of whatever sort; for triplicity proceeds from
an affirming, as it were reconciling, unifying, fulfilling, har-
monious viewpoint. Time has two dimensions, because it
corresponds to the transforming, limiting principle manifested by duality, of whatever sort; for duality proceeds
from an irreconcilable, separating, in itself dissatisfied and
insufficient, questioning viewpoint. For this reason, for example, the sexes cannot coexist without being united and
liberated through a third element—love and their common
fruit. Similarly, day and night cannot exist simultaneously,
except through and in a third element, namely, morning
or evening. Two eyes or ears find their third element in a
common perception; two hands in a united expression of
will.

Duality is the creator of all manifestation. Before and
above all manifestation is the one Principle that suffices
unto Itself and is Unique and Total. In order that it may repeat itself in mirror images, and realise itself anew in these
repetitions, ever and without end, the unnameable, boundlessly sovereign Self, above all determinations, must, as
all-real Non-Being or Beyond-Being, clothe itself in Being, which distinguishes itself from Beyond-Being in that,
though determined by nothing, it determines itself. Now,
in this Being lies particularised existence. Existence is
divided—not as such, but from the standpoint of manifestation whose provenance we seek to explain—into quin-

94

tessence and *materia prima*; primordial fire and primordial water. Out of this duality is born manifestation, which is the fabric of all worlds.

*

Just as numerical unity sets itself in opposition to multiplicity, and is the latter's centre, so, too, is spiritual Unity the Centre of the possibilities of manifestation; it is the one Possibility as such—Being.

*

The ancients did not have extensively elaborated doctrinal books, but they read what the moderns construct with many words, in books that strike the moderns as simple and meaningless. What modern man can only laboriously describe, ancient man read between the lines; what the moderns express in a hundred words, the ancients understood in one. Only a little had to come from outside to awaken his Knowledge, for he had most of his learning within himself. For modern man, almost everything has to come from outside, because he has forgotten the inner science.

*

The sufficient reason for exercising the will can only come from Knowledge. Knowledge is one, and men are one in Knowledge, not only symbolically, but also in fact. The purpose of exercising the will can only be Knowledge. Being is inwardly all luminous, all Knowledge; and Omnipotence is only an aspect of Being; it is in a sense its expression, its Word, its spouse, but not its ultimate and highest Essence; for power does not suffice unto itself as Knowledge does: rather, it has its origin and its end in Knowledge—it is the manifestation of Knowledge. He whose knowledge is in the flesh has a strong body; he

95

whose knowledge is in his intellect has power though the Spirit.

The Intellect is one; the intellect that understands a truth cannot be an intellect other than the one that understands this truth; for it is the same as the truth. But what in no way differs is one and the same thing, just as light through which an object becomes visible is no different to one eye than to another, but remains one and the same light.

*

To the extent that the spiritual seeker has in him individualistic elements such as sentiments, he cannot eliminate these; for hatred of individualism is also a sentiment, and it cannot elevate him above his sentiments. Rather, the individualistic elements must be dammed and channelled in the direction in which they should flow. They must be able to serve in defence against sentiments which could oppose spiritualisation: so long as the directed sentiment thus moves towards transformation and re-evaluation, knowledge must permeate, dilate and dissolve it, and turn its energy to account. The way of Knowledge is a way of Unity and a way to Unity: reason is unitive in its nature, but the Spirit is truly one. Sentiment, however, is multiple, and must be unified in ultimate Love. Since knowledge and will are revelations of the unfragmented Spirit, they must in a certain sense have negating, limiting effects in fragmented reality, whereas the effect of sentiment and desire seems positive and expanding, but is in fact illusory.

In one sense man must unify completely; in another sense he must separate decisively. He must gather into unity all the contents of knowledge and will on the principial plane; and separate all their exteriorizations in manifestation, in order to fulfil each one completely.

Thus he must in principle determine reason and sentiment unitively, but keep them separate in fact.

In meditation on the Divine, reason is a mere tool for man in the expression of Knowledge: he does not fall prey to reason's limits, as do those who see it as an end in itself. He determines reason on the basis of the Spirit, in order that it ultimately dissolve—not in the irrational, but in the supra-rational; just as he does not dissolve sentiment in that which contradicts it, but in that which is its ultimate fulfilment.

Whereas primordial meditation is a spiritual meeting with the Divine and proceeds from the core of our being in which we ourselves are divine, so that actually the Divine speaks and reason only perceives, prayer is an individually limited meeting with the Divine, which proceeds only from within the "I", in which we are not divine but different from the Divine; so that we speak to the Divine with our limited capacities, and as ourselves, thus also with our sentiment—not as that which we can be through Knowledge. In meditation man is a stranger to himself, because the Spirit shining through reason is distinct from man, and determines him in order to spiritualise him; in prayer man is a stranger to the Spirit, because prayer has its meaning in man and of course comes from man, so as to create a protective and strengthening climate in which meditation is not exposed to anything hostile and is not distracted.

Before meditation, as before prayer, man must forget all else. After meditation or prayer he must forget them, so that he is not absorbed or possessed by the mere contents of his consciousness; and so that meditation and prayer can act beyond his waking consciousness. For what enters man, as in meditation, and what emerges from him, as in prayer, must pass through form; not in order that he fall prey to form—which as such is always limited and diverse—

97

but in order that he recognize its relativity and overcome it.

The one primordial doctrine shattered, the more it was given expression and the less men partook in its spirit. The forms in which it continues to live must be diverse—otherwise they would not be forms, but pure Spirit. Now, the doctrinal forms which proceeded from meditation remained conscious of their formal state, and also recognised the Spirit in the other forms of the primordial doctrine; but those that proceeded from prayer were confused with their formality, and saw the Spirit in it and thus not in other forms, least of all in those which arose not from prayer but from meditation. There are two sources of doctrinal authority or infallibility: an outer one, which confirms the actual provenance of the primordial doctrine; and an inner one, which is based on the revelation of the Spirit through direct Knowledge. The outer source is, as such, only relatively veracious, but it is incontestably reliable within this relativity. The inner source is, in its essence, Truth itself, and therefore inordinately more important than the outer source, just as a man's own direct participation in the Spirit is more important than that handed down by Tradition—though the former has need of the latter in order to be effective. The inner source of infallibility can, however, break through the outer source, as Jesus—in the Name of the Spirit and as proclaimer of the primordial doctrine, although within particular but necessary formal preconditions—broke through the outer source: namely, the Judaic tradition. At the same time, because of his concordance with the Envoys of God, he referred to this tradition, and thus confirmed his connection with the primordial doctrine.

He whose spirit stands on the ground of the primordial doctrine has power over its forms, just as he who has ideas also has power over words. But he who stands on the ground of traditional form alone has no power over the inner Source, except through arrogation, for he knows only form, not the primordial doctrine.

*

Just as the body becomes everything that it consumes, and must return to the earth, because it lives from the earth, so the soul must return to illusion to the extent that it lives from illusion. He whose cognition lives only from the most external and ephemeral will not transcend the limitations of his nature. He who does not respond to one call from Knowledge, will also not respond to a thousand calls, and a time will come for him when there is no further call from Knowledge soliciting an answer; and then the simple truth the man heard without hearing it, or saw without seeing it, departs and leaves him to fall into his error, for when man no longer participates even in the fragmented reflection of the inner Source, nothing remains to him but himself, as husk and negation. Truth will abandon the doubter and vacillator, as the sun departs from the earth and leaves it behind, massive and cold.

Man has unlimited power, for he has all the power that exists, and power is unlimited; but he does not know he has it, that it is there and is unlimited; for man's existence is ignorance, and power is the expression of knowledge.

*

All revelations, like all scriptural sayings and all testimony of the Spirit in general, have several meanings which do not mutually exclude each other, but rather complement each other to form one teaching that encompasses the most diverse domains. The purely historical meaning of a scriptural saying is in no way opposed to its meaning on a higher plane, any more than the historical Envoy of God is opposed to his universal and purely spiritual meaning—whose human manifestation he is—or to his symbolical connection with the sun or fire.

The same is true for the doctrinal form in which the Spirit is transmitted and kept alive for a part of humanity; the literal sense, which is absolutely necessary for the form, and thus for the preservation of the Spirit—be it only a diminished preservation—cannot contradict eternal Truth, of which it is a reflection and a fragmented aspect; nor can it prevent that a meaning proceeding from the letter and from the general formal expression transcend the literal, formal, and dissolve it in its outward meaning or necessary application to society. Wherefore this meaning of the form cannot be incorporated, since it signifies a danger for doctrine and its preservation because of the ignorance of the majority; thus the doctrine's inner meaning, protected by the letter, must be entrusted to those who not only grasp it without harm, but who can also realise it as a signpost to the formless spirituality of the eternal primordial doctrine. Were one to object that the inner meaning of a tradition opposes its literal meaning and its social consequences, one would be forgetting that Truth itself contradicts its possible forms to a certain extent, precisely in that it is more than everything formal; and that nevertheless the relatively falsified form is necessary for the expression of Truth, and for its capacity to live in certain conditions, and does not arise from human will; and that this relative outward falsification must penetrate more deeply in the case of doctrinal forms stemming from an orientation to prayer and not pure meditation. Thus it is apparent that prayer comes from man and has its purpose in man, whereas meditation comes from the Spirit and has its meaning in the Spirit.

A sacred Word has all the meaning it can have, and excludes none. Similarly sayings of Jesus gainsay exoterists, who deny the infallibility of the inner source and its right to exist, just as they deny everything that transcends the outermost, literal sense—and everything that extends and is valid beyond form.

Power is nothing but manifested Spirit, just as Spirit can also be called principial Power, with the reservation that the Spirit as such is not power and has no need of it, just as the Essence does not need to be justified by substance. If power is, in its principle, Spirit, and Spirit is, in its manifestation, power, this distinction exists in the Spirit's first image—Being—only insofar as one considers Being either in the sense of its truth or in the sense of its reality. Knowledge flowing into the heart through the Spirit answers perceptions flowing in through the senses, through its manifestation as will; the will is a particular activity directed outwards, while desire is nothing but a loss of will determined from outside—a submission to phenomena. The Spirit is one: if the will answers the Spirit instead of the latter's fragmented reflections, it goes beyond or through phenomena, and answers the one Essence hidden in the diverse, the many. The will thereby becomes one, like the Spirit; the spell of the phenomenal world is pierced and dissolved; ignorance, which hardened and weighed down the heart, is vanquished; and the pure Spirit shines again in its original sovereignty, alone and divine and absolutely free from all limitations, completely absorbed by ultimate Reality and distinct from it in nothing.

*

The ordinary concept of knowledge means above all a distinction, a determination of the knowing faculty from outside, being affected by something else that is differentiated from its surroundings by some characteristic. The knowledge of God is the experience of His Uniqueness through

101

Itself; but God's Self-Contemplation can be compared only symbolically to the ordinary process of knowledge, so that it is simply out of conceptual need that God's Reality can be said to be the content or object of His knowledge. The distinction between knowledge and reality exists only because of the limitation of fragmented knowledge, since the latter is insufficient to attain the one Reality, and is unable to overcome the divisive and destructive tendency inherent in fragmented existence.

The universe is one circle of knowledge or one state of consciousness. The earthly world of created beings is another: it disintegrates anew into countless further circles or states, right down to the knowing faculty of each individual, or even to the single temporally limited individual cognition of an individual faculty. The world is a state of consciousness, split up a thousandfold and repeating itself a thousandfold, glittering in countless variations. These self-replications of the universal state of consciousness are graduated upward to the unfragmented grasp of Reality. The horizontal planes ascending from the foundation of a pyramid, one on top of the other, becoming narrower towards the apex—planes of unlimited number, since they have no vertical dimension—symbolise the innumerable general states of consciousness that divide themselves into cells that are likewise innumerable because they are dimensionless: the latter signify the individual phenomena of such planes of consciousness. The apex of the pyramid is then the dimensionless point which touches and as it were sucks in the Immeasurable, transforming it into manifestation, which is realised inversely and by involution.

But that Immeasurability is pure light. On entering through the apex of the cosmic pyramid, it is darkened, it is transposed into fragmented or coloured light. It then spreads out over the first planes of consciousness and disperses into the innumerable cells which again break and transform it. The planes from the unextended apex to any horizontally extended plane, however close they still seem to be relative to the apex, are countless; for if the transition from the plane considered lowest to another plane is endlessly divisible into further planes, there can be no actual transition from the dimensionless to that which has dimensions, any more than there can be a transition from Being to that which exists.

The world is a state of consciousness: it is thus a state of cognition. From the apex of the symbolical pyramid to the base, cognition becomes darkened. What shines through the apex to the base is Knowledge. The outermost cells of cognition live from Knowledge. Each cognitive cell is connected with the apex of the pyramid by a straight line. Innumerable rays go from the apex to the base; the central ray runs through the centre of all planes to the base, and thus dominates each plane from the centre. Hence one can say: the centre is the Envoy of God or the Son of God; the ray is the Holy Spirit; the apex is the divine Generator or Father; the planes are the outer doctrinal sources, every point on the plane a reflection of the Word— a man—and every ray a reflection of the Holy Spirit, or a particular revelation of the Holy Spirit through the inner doctrinal source. The rays clustered around the central ray correspond to the inner doctrinal source, insofar as their endpoint actually participates in this source; the further the rays distance themselves from the central ray, the more indirect this participation becomes, because the ray reaches its endpoint only by an oblique route. The participation of the ordinary man in the inner source of knowing remains *de facto* merely a principial possibility.

The apex of the pyramid can signify the quintessence, and the base *materia prima*. Thus the edges also signify either the actual or the quintessential application of the apex to dimension; and the side surfaces bounded by

103

the edges signify the actual or material application of the apex. Similarly, each horizontal plane is framed by vertices and boundary lines, for its limitation must be at the same time principial and actual, essential and material: that is, the principial duality represented by apex and base must repeat itself in edges and surfaces as manifested duality. The pyramid is an extension of the miracle that is consummated in the contact between the apex and the first plane. As stated, the centre of every plane corresponds to the Envoy of God, the Master or Lawgiver, or the Word as such.

The tiniest fragments of the pyramid are connected with its apex, just as the most limited states of consciousness are connected with pure Knowledge. A sensory impression participates in pure Knowledge through the faculty of perception, which participates along with the other senses in the intelligence: the intelligence, constituting the centre where the senses meet, participates in Knowledge through its connection with the heart, the inner instrument of Knowledge and seat of the Intellect. From the heart, which receives Reality, the knowledge of Reality radiates into the brain and is transformed into concepts and thoughts, which take their form and external motivations from outwardly perceptible sensory reality, through the portals of the senses. When we said that the heart is the seat of the Intellect, this is not to imply that the Intellect is contained and enclosed in the heart; but rather that the heart is the instrument of knowledge, sensitive to the radiations of the one limitless Spirit, just as the eye is to physical light and the ear to physical vibrations. But what the faculties bring as something fragmented, shattered to the intelligence, whose seat is in the brain, the heart brings as something unitive, whole—to the degree that it is receptive to spiritual light or spiritual vibrations. The brain is the centre of man as such; the heart is his centre as

104

a complete being. The brain is his discriminating centre, his hallmark, through which he is man; the heart constitutes his synthesizing, unifying centre, through which he is divine. In the brain man's *Weltanschauung* is manifested through the two kinds of knowledge of Reality: the exterior-sensory, and the interior-spiritual. The heart is the indivisible, divine Eye, the senses the fragmented, splintered eye; the integral knowledge of the heart flows in a generalising, determining, unifying way into the hollow perceptions of the senses, and transforms them into concepts. Men tend either toward the senses or toward the heart, either towards phenomena or towards Being; and consequently they live either in sentiments and imagination, or in reason and memory. But whereas reason receives its determination from the Spirit and employs memory only for its own manifestation, and just as the essence has need of substance for its manifestation, so, too, the sentiments are determined by phenomena—thus by nothing principial, but by the merely factual. And consequently they do not transpose essence into diversity in order to lead these phenomena back to Unity: they transpose it into merely factual, mutable elements like sentiments, and thus scatter what was unified into diversity again.

He whose heart is dull defines phenomena with little knowledge: thus he has insufficient or wrong concepts and allows them to be determined by facts. But dullness or acuity of the senses has no meaning for the Spirit, because the factual is without significance for the principial.

Through direct participation in the Spirit man is conscious of the Spirit and of the dependence and relativity of reason; through indirect participation he is enclosed in reason; thus are sages distinguished from mere thinkers.

With respect to what the senses convey, a being responds only according to the receptivity of his heart, either

105

to direct phenomenal reality or the Reality transmitted by it. His will is thus either splintered like phenomenal reality or unified like the Reality which is expressed and at the same time veiled by phenomenal reality.

The five senses signify a fivefold symbolism of, and at the same time a fivefold deviation from, pure Reality: this deviation is the consequence of a hardening of the heart, an estrangement, through which the heart receives only a diminished radiation of the Spirit. But the merely factual centre-point of man is in his brain; it is his sixth or central sense, and constitutes everything that is called the soul. For this reason overcoming the world means overcoming the soul, the "I", the brain; because a rich man shall hardly enter into the kingdom of God, and we must enter through the strait gate.

The heart is the lost Eden in us or the lost primordial doctrine, the lost Word, the forgotten Name of God, the estranged exile returning at the end of the world. The consequence of the impulse outwards, the search for the false Eden outside the heart, the answering to lesser reality, was the disintegration of Consciousness into knowledge and will, which are inseparably one in the Divine. The forms of creatures correspond to the things of the senses to which they were drawn in order to find the lost Eden. The senses rule over creatures, and thus the heart is submerged, and is from the human standpoint devoid of reason, but nonetheless the centre of all creatures. In this fact is manifested the contradiction that the human "I" does not lie in man's centre, and yet is the centre of human consciousness. This consciousness, like the "I" and everything human, lies in the ephemeral. Every creature symbolizes spiritual glimmering: God makes possible, and maintains, the world, but He is not in it: He is indeed its ultimate Cause, but not its direct, limiting wellspring.

For the ordinary man the brain, thus ignorance and doubt, are the spiritual centre; for the spiritual man the heart, thus certitude and Unity, are the spiritual centre. For this reason the spiritual man has dissolved his "I", he has entered into the "I" of every being, he has found the Self, which is one and lies in the heart. This overcoming of the "I" is expressed in the saying, "Love thy neighbour as thyself."

*

The knowledge that the Spirit is free encompasses the knowledge that the non-spiritual is not free.

He who acknowledges the freedom of the Spirit must also acknowledge the servitude of the flesh: if he wants to be free in the flesh, he must also disavow the freedom of the Spirit.

He whose heart is receptive and irradiated by the Spirit defines the radiations of the senses according to the consciousness he has of the Spirit: since the Spirit is one, It determines phenomena unitively. Man's will is then unitive, like his knowledge and like the Spirit.

Man is a consciousness with respect to the Spirit, and an existence with respect to Reality. If his heart is sound, his consciousness returns to the Spirit, and his will to Reality. His consciousness returns as it were to the Centre and his will to the present moment.

The will has its meaning uniquely and solely in Knowledge.

*

A form is never convincing in itself, nor does a word in itself ever have the power of proof; the need for causality differs according to people and times. A form becomes convincing by being in accordance with the inner Source of conviction; a word has the power of proof when the light of the inner Source of proof falls on it. Everything that can be put forward to justify the formal can do so only in a relative manner.

In the Scriptures there are no contradictions, only different viewpoints whose expressions seem contradictory to those who stop short at the formal, or whose minds are corrosive: they do not seek to understand anything, only to deny, negate and destroy.

*

Consciousness means delimitation. The limitless is supraconscious; limits are unconscious. Every thought and every movement is a delimitation, a consciousness that inwardly recalls the Limitless and is outwardly limited.

Every thought is simultaneously a delimitation and an extension; it is also either one or the other.

THIRD COLLECTION

Written *anno* 1932 in Basel, Lausanne and Marseilles

WE ARE IN ALL THAT WE KNOW—and all that we know is in us. There can be no doubt that we know, for even he who claims that we can know nothing, or that we cannot even know nothing, already proceeds from multiple cognitions. Otherwise it would be impossible for him not only to make his erroneous claims, but also even to move, to walk, indeed to live; for there is no doubter who, for the sake of consistency, would disdain to make use of his knowledge; otherwise he could not distinguish a loaf from a stone. Therefore he must admit that he knows, at least relatively; for, were no knowledge to enter him, no reaction could issue from him, and he could not act; every action is a determination proceeding from a discernment, and every discernment presupposes knowledge and is knowledge. But just as we admit that knowledge, however limited and relative, nonetheless exists, there is no sufficient reason to impose conceptual restrictions on this knowledge, other than the narrowness of those who boast of their ignorance and call themselves doubters in order to evade all knowledge that transcends the human and its needs, and in particular the consequences of such pure knowledge. For nothing is easier than to gainsay what transcends us, the consequences of which can be binding on us. But being bound by the Spirit is true freedom.

Man is originally a recognizer, a knower; his intentional limiting of his knowledge and consequently his will spells ruin and degeneration; and thus conceptual doubt is also artificial, it is nothing innate in man, nothing immediately enlightening. Actual doubt is an actual ignorance, a weakness of the spirit; principial doubt is a principial ignorance, a disease of the spirit, a madness.

To think is one thing; "to-be-thought" another. Very few think, for it is they who "are thought". There is no true relation between them and their thoughts; for they

111

do not know themselves. Neither is there a true relation between their thoughts and the objects thereof, for their thoughts do not know what they are. For the thinking man, thoughts are not their own objects, and he himself is not his thoughts.

*

We eat, we drink, we sleep. However we do not live from these alone.

For man shall not live by bread alone, but by every word that proceedeth out of the mouth of God.

We eat because it is day, we sleep because it is night. We could not live without day and night.

But from what should we live, if not from bread alone? We should live from this, from that, according to the word from the mouth of God that touched us. And we should live according to this word in the same way as we live from food, drink and sleep—and are governed by day and night, the rising and setting of the sun.

All movement, from the most significant to the most minuscule, is borne upon vibration.

Now, he who doubts spiritual nourishment and imagines he is able to escape the worship God has imposed upon us as law, forgets that this worship is not only man's original predisposition, but implicates every man, whether or not he denies it; that every omitted testimony to the Spirit is not mere omission, but at the same time a testimony to the appearance, the illusion, the error which man worships. Nobody can be unwilling to worship, for he would thus fall into contradiction with himself: for every house that is divided against itself falls.

Thus all men pray. But some know that they worship and what they worship and are one with their original determination, whereas others do not know that they

112

worship, nor what they worship, and they are at variance with their original determination.

*

Thoughts and actions arise from intentions. But what is the nature of these intentions? They are manifestations of ignorance, which is indistinguishable from suffering. Thus all thoughts, which are inner actions, and all actions, which are transposed thoughts, negate, insofar as they come from what is merely human; but they affirm, insofar as they come from the Spirit.

For the masses there are sins which must be avoided on grounds of conscience; and thus the masses believe in virtues. For the spiritual man there are only shortcomings, ruptures of equilibrium, errors, inversions, which must be avoided for reasons of consistency; he believes in no virtue, but rather in spiritual outlook, participation in the Spirit, which through its preponderance and its emergence in man, radiates through all man's inward and outward manifestations and permits that he participate in the Spirit, so that the complete man is absorbed into the spiritual and therefore resurrected into the one Spirit from the thousandfold death of error—as Christ was resurrected in the Spirit from the death of the flesh, and as the flesh of Enoch, Elias and Mary was taken up and absorbed by the Spirit.

Man sins or errs because his heart is crippled; he hears without hearing and sees without seeing. He believes he wants the spiritual, but he does not want it and cannot want it to the extent that he does not know it.

When a man asks why he should want the spiritual and nothing outside the spiritual, let a fire be fanned into flames for him, into which he holds his hand, and let it be said to him: outside the Spirit there is only ignorance, and ignorance is nothing but this fire. If man does not wish to

113

burn even his hand, how much less should he wish to burn there completely, and not just bodily, but in all that makes him man. And how can he not want the Spirit and nothing except the Spirit, if everything else is not of the Spirit, but of ignorance and fire, of suffering?

The individual's acts respond to his perception. Life responds to the heart's knowledge. In other words: an action responds to the knowledge of a particular fact, life responds to our general and innate knowledge of Reality. Just as love results from the knowledge of the beautiful, or defence from the knowledge of attack, so life proceeds from a particular knowledge of Reality. Life is therefore ignorance, for if it were pure Knowing it would also be pure Reality and Joy.

*

For most people, the individual man is no mere debris of the one Spirit, but a sovereign, eternal being. The Spirit is thought of as multiple because the Scriptural sentence, "In my Father's house there are many mansions" is misunderstood. But this means: not every being enters into God in such a way that he is dissolved in Him and is no longer distinct from Him: many remain in the outer heavenly circles.

*

Let what is finite remain finite; for what must be infinite is already infinite.

What are thoughts and actions? They are impotent attempts to realise the Infinite within the finite; they are attempts by the finite to become infinite. The finite wants to become infinite because it does not know that it is ultimately infinite and that its finiteness is based on this ignorance alone. The finite has ears to hear and hears not; eyes to see and sees not; it knows the Divine without

114

knowing it; thus the finite wants to become equal with the Divine and affirm itself, spread, glorify itself, but without giving itself up; the finite wants to be divine as something finite; and because it is actually in one sense divine, it has joy, sovereignty and reality—otherwise it could not even be finite, or be at all; but because it is not the Divine, it has suffering and impotence, it is unreal. Thus what is made manifest is simultaneously a paean to the Divine and a revolt against the Divine.

Grasping this truth dissolves what is hardened, conglomerated, dense, and can be compared to evaporation in space; or to being in this truth as in water, flowing and always unifying itself. This truth leads into the centre of all things and liberates us from the illusory, seemingly unique centre of the "I". Through its orientation to this truth the world is in the Divine. The way to this truth and the world's redemption is an immersion in the inevitable, is total resignation to the divine Will, which is revealed by the determinations that distinguish the being from the rest of the world and in a certain sense make him unique. This truth dissolves from within, it penetrates, it percolates into all the pores of the hardened man. For in the heart of every pore is pure peace, pure joy, pure innocence, pure goodness, pure beauty, in measureless plenitude. In the interior of things are lightness and fragrance, nothing contradictory, nothing violent, nothing restrictive, nothing negating, no hardness, no hatred, no conflict, only equilibrium and harmony. The spirit of the Centre is sober and tranquil, cool and imperturbable like the eternal laws. In the centre of man is woman, and were he to know this completely, he would seek woman no more; in the interior is salvation, is the unifying, is sweetness. In the interior is pure affirmation, pure love. Phenomena are affirmation which is disintegrating; they affirm through their existence, but they negate their existence by the very fact of existing. The

115

considered, apportioned, serene, comes from the interior; from it come correct proportions, correct structure, symmetry, vibration. Therefore he who has dissolved himself and is thus divided amongst all beings and so to speak spreads himself over the whole world, yet has no "here", no "I"—he accepts without protest the divine determinations which are imposed upon him as his particular law and in fact proceed from his own state of mind.

All things grow out of this resignation. No being can arise by force; rather, he must ripen slowly, he must draw deep breath, he must unfold in total submission to eternal laws. This submission is the divine Presence in phenomena, just as dimension is the presence of the centre in things or an application of the centre to things. Insofar as man is finite and must take the finite into account, he can do nothing other and nothing better than to resign himself to his finiteness, understand it, know it in the sense that he no longer seek to realise the Infinite in the finite, and that he sink into the inevitable without concupiscence and inebriation, emptying only the cup of his existence. Through this resignation he finds in himself Woman, who saves and appeases him. He shall be poured out like rain over the whole earth; he shall see through his passionless centre and contemplate the centre in each phenomenon, and this centre shall be his centre, and his centre shall be the centre of every phenomenon. This Centre is the healing power, the blessing, that vanquishes all evil.

But insofar as man is infinite, namely in the pure Spirit, whose entrance is the heart, he cannot in any way know anything but the one pure Infinite. If the standpoint of resignation contains a triplicity, the standpoint opposed to it is dual; for whereas the standpoint explained above is based upon the ternary: infinity, finiteness and reconciliation between the two, the other standpoint is based only upon the irreconcilable duality of Spirit and illusion,

116

Being and non-being, Reality and appearance. This other standpoint arises from the negation of Reality in phenomena. Therefore this standpoint, as opposed to the previous affirming aspect, can be called the negating aspect, though this has a meaning only with respect to manifestation, that is, what exists, what is present. This negating aspect, whose symbolism lies in time, just as that of the affirming aspect lies in space, is exclusive and unique; it leads man back to the pure Spirit and burns phenomena through It; he sees as Spirit and sees nothing but Spirit. Just as the participation of phenomena in the Divine means resignation and peace, the non-participation of phenomena in the Divine means non-resignation, revolt and conflict. This non-participation is the limiting, dividing, separating, negating, the determining opposed to the infinite, it is fire opposed to water; for whereas fire can only be one unique fire, but is always completely fire, water can be water in many ways and is never exclusively water.

He who resigns himself to Unity, like a little child who clings to his mother's breast, seems great. He seems great, but he is not, for his greatness is the greatness of Unity; only Unity—the ultimate, profound—is great.

*

Sanctifying grace is nothing but an inflow of knowledge. Without knowledge man cannot want anything; and were he to want God without knowledge, his will would be meaningless. Man cannot want God without knowing Him in the measure of this willing; for without knowledge this will would have no sufficient reason.

No Envoy of God would have recounted parables had he thought that man could come to God other than through knowledge; he would only have given orders. Nor, therefore, has anyone taught that Truth depends only on the exterior proofs of his message.

117

To know the Spirit is to know that there is only Spirit and nothing but Spirit.

To will the Spirit is to will nothing but Spirit and to will everything in the Spirit.

Man cannot act against his faith. His faith is his vocation and his law. Man is fruitful only where he believes. Without faith he deceives himself and others.

*

What is in the heart is an obstacle to the Spirit's penetration of man; the phenomena and events which surround man correspond to what is in his heart.

Man stands in the world in a twofold manner: in the positive, expanding sense through phenomena, in the negative, contracting sense through events. Phenomena determine his knowledge, events determine his will; his knowledge distinguishes and vanquishes phenomena, and simultaneously his will unifies and vanquishes events.

*

Man should always be twofold: on the one hand a warrior and a victor, and on the other hand a priest and a sacrificer. He must despise and fight, yet simultaneously love and bless.

Man must reckon with evil without fearing it, and with good without expecting it.

*

The Divine is the cause. Everything affirmative is Its consequence. The negating is Its consequence only insofar as it is negated affirmation; only thus can the false, bad, weak, ugly also be Its consequence. Negation exists because in the Divine lies the possibility of an apparent negation of Its Reality; this possibility is an expression of Its All-Possibility. The Divine is pure affirmation; pure

118

negation cannot exist, for nothing can be opposed to the Divine, and what seems to be Its opposite is so only relatively and apparently. For were something entirely Its opposite, it could not even be, since Being is the unitary aspect of the Divine. The opposite of the Divine would be nothingness, but nothingness is nothing; it can operate only very conditionally as an expression of the divine All-Possibility, as a diminution, never as a pure negation; it can reduce Reality to the gross physical world, where it becomes powerless and cannot negate any further; thus the gross physical world is the limit of the negating possibility of nothingness, which does not exist as such. But if it cannot reduce Reality any further than the gross physical world, where its possibility of reduction for our earthly existence stops, it can still, within this final and most extreme reckoning, further fragment its debris; through this arises the negation within negation, namely the false, bad, weak, ugly—which inward fragmentation is made manifest not only in the physical domain, but also in that of the soul, of which the physical domain is nothing but the effect and the outermost delimitation.

Therefore nothingness cannot be, for if it could, it would be a divinity. But there is only one Divine, in It is no duality, and Its All-Reality surpasses even Its Unity.

*

The Divine, the highest Principle, is infinite, and infinite are its possibilities. Its Infinity can thus exclude no possibility, not even that of impossibility, namely, nothingness; but this possibility of the contradictory, unreal, cannot be possible in the All-Reality of the Divine itself: it is therefore apparently possible outside and below the Divine and realises itself as world. The world is nothing but the manifestation of the possibility of the contradictory, unreal, impossible; hence the world is the spectacle of the All cor-

119

roded by nothingness, of Reality shattered by unreality, of negated affirmation, of limited infinity. But because unreality, the nothingness of the Divine, is impossible, yet in a certain way possible within and in consequence of Its All-Possibility, Being was conceived as first hint, so to speak, of nothingness, and as first manifestation of this possibility, and seeped away into two poles, one masculine and one feminine, in order to give birth to nothingness, so far as this is possible within Reality, that is, possible at all. And thus Being gave birth to the Spirit, and through the Spirit, to the universe. Universal manifestation is the uniquely possible reality of unreality and as such not in the Divine; but were it not somehow in the Divine as possibility, divine All-Possibility would not be infinite.

Being divided in two and gave birth to the universe. As perceptible world, the manifestation of the Spirit became barren; for were the perceptible world fecund, nothingness would arise from it, and nothingness is not possible, because Being cannot be non-being and nothing is outside Being, except the highest divine Principle, which veils Itself in Being. Therefore nothingness is possible only insofar as it can be represented through Being. What can be thus represented cannot be nothingness as such, for this does not exist, only its possibility; but the latter is not consummate, for the Divine alone is consummate.

This possibility of contradiction with itself lies in the divine All-Possibility as does the point in measureless space.

For the ignorant man the world is like measureless space, filled with unrestricted possibilities; for him God is like the fixed point. For the spiritual man the world is like the point, which has only one possibility; for him the Divine is like measureless space, in which he loses himself in primordial free flight and is extinguished, like a star as morning approaches.

*

In its centre, every thing ceases to be what it is; but precisely through this it begins to be.

*

All doing is the consequence of a love that is separated from its object. This is why spiritual love engenders no doing, for the Spirit is none other than its Love.

*

From the spiritual point of view we are knowledge; from the human, will. Now, since we are, if we are spiritual, nothing but knowledge, neither must we, insofar as we are human, be anything other than will; but will is never an end in itself, rather, it is an emanation of knowledge. Thus the will must flow back into its sufficient reason, by no longer being distinct from it, by no longer being other than knowledge.

*

Man does not live from bread alone—whether he knows it or not, whether he wishes it or not. When nourishing himself, he also eats either knowledge or ignorance. All necessary doing is sacred; but one must know what one is doing, and do everything in the Spirit.

*

The world is a silken pall, in which lies a king, rigid and deeply enshrouded. He loves the silk in which he is wrapped, without knowing that it is a shroud, his shroud, and that beyond this shroud extends a whole living world with an immeasurable heaven. He does not want to rend the shroud, nor shatter his gilded sarcophagus, because he loves it.

Every man is this enshrouded, buried king.

121

*

It is the Nameless, Ungraspable; the Hidden-behind-a-thousand-veils. If one seeks to grasp It, It withdraws. If one seeks to think It, It seals the understanding. It shatters him who knows It.

*

At sunrise the stars fade away. Thus do all things fade away when the Spirit rises.

In the brightness of day one has no need of a lamp. Therefore the Spirit has no need of reason.

*

There is no kingdom that is closest to the Divine, and none that is furthest from it. Nowhere does there exist a relation to the Divine.

*

All is dream. The world drains away. I alone am eternal, nameless, inconceivable.

*

Awakening lies in the present moment. Behold only the One, and behold the One totally. Lay hold on nothing—be held by nothing, Existence is a dream; everything is in primordial Being, solitary, high, ungraspable.

*

We are what we will.

*

He who grasps that the pleasures of this world are not of this world, has grasped much.

*

Everything in the life of the spiritual man is afloat upon his immersion in the Divine, like specks of dust upon deep waters. Life is light, only immersion is heavy; and even its heaviness is made light for the spiritual man.

Days and nights follow one another like breaths; breaths follow one another like days and nights. As life is borne by days and nights, so immersion is borne by breaths; life flows through days and nights, and the Spirit flows through breaths. Breath is the body of immersion, of primordial meditation. Breath dissolves the body and transforms it into spirit. In order for the Spirit to go through breath, breath must go through the Spirit. Breath is the sacred fire that purifies and transforms man.

*

Outwardly there is action, will and knowledge. Inwardly only will and knowledge remain. And in the innermost there is only knowledge.

Action is only an emanation of will, not distinct from it, just as the world is only an emanation of Omnipotence.

Knowledge, will and action are but an image of Infinity, Reality and manifestation. Will abides without action, it is the cause of action. Knowledge abides without will, it is the cause of will, just as quintessence, essentiality or the primordial fire abide without their plane of manifestation, materiality or primordial water, and just as man was before woman and has meaning without woman.

Reality is none other than All-Possibility, thus Possibility as such. That which is not real is also not possible, thus it is not at all. All-Reality must also contain the reality of the unreal, namely the world. In other words, All-Possibility must also contain the possibility of the impossible, its contradiction, even if this can only be apparent; for otherwise it would not be All-Possibility, it would not be Reality.

*

Space is the Centre that is mirrored and manifested in height, breadth and depth. We escape the Centre in order to find the Centre; this is why we are in space. We are in the Centre and do not know it, thus we have lost it. All that occurs in space arises from the Centre and returns to the Centre; it is simultaneously an exodus and a return.

Time is the present moment that is mirrored and manifested in the past and the future. We escape the present moment in order to find it; this is why we are in time. We are in the present moment and do not know it; thus we have lost it. All that occurs in time arises from the present and returns to the present; it is simultaneously an exodus and a return.

Number is Unity that is mirrored and manifested in multiplicity. We escape Unity in order to find it; this is why we are in number. We are in Unity and do not know it; thus we have lost it. All that occurs in number arises from Unity and returns to Unity; it is simultaneously an exodus and a return.

Form is perfection that is mirrored and manifested in diversity. We escape perfection in order to find it; this is why we are in form. We are in perfection and do not know it; thus we have lost it. All that occurs in form arises from perfection and returns to perfection; it is simultaneously an exodus and a return.

Life is pleasure that is mirrored and manifested in desire. We escape pleasure in order to find it; this is why we are in life. We are in pleasure and do not know it; thus we have lost it. Everything that occurs in life arises from pleasure and returns to pleasure, it is simultaneously an exodus and a return.

124

Were the centre not a fragmented centre, space would not arise from it. In space there is only dimension, however endless. But the Divine is pure Centre, hence It is infinite.

Were the present not a fragmented present, time would not arise from it. In time there is only duration, however perpetual. But the Divine is pure Present, hence It is eternal.

Were unity not fragmented unity, number would not arise from it. In number there is only multiplicity, however countless. But the Divine is pure Unity, hence It is all.

Were perfection not fragmented perfection, form would not arise from it. In form there is only symbolism or resemblance, however unsurpassable. But the Divine is pure perfection or Selfhood, for it is undetermined and Itself.

Were pleasure not fragmented pleasure, life would not arise from it. In life there is only passion, however satisfying. But the Divine is pure Pleasure, hence it is All-Joy.

*

The forms of created beings correspond to the things toward which they were attracted in order to find the lost Eden, and to the way in which they sought it.

The reality of the phenomenal world lies in the "I", and the "I" repeats itself endlessly; in this is manifested the contradictoriness of fragmented reality: it has many centre-points and only one circumference.

*

Four things are sacred: love, struggle, suffering and death.

*

There is a return to the Divine through the quintessence and a return through *materia prima*; in the first case

125

the spiritual man proceeds from his quintessence, the Spirit, and negates the non-spiritual, the illusory; this is the standpoint of the Principle. In the other case the spiritual man proceeds from what is closest to him, from what is immediately given, and affirms its respective centre; this is the standpoint of manifestation. Every manifestation is the rupture of an equilibrium; the centre of every manifestation is its equilibrium. But this centre is again a manifestation, thus a rupture of equilibrium in transformable *materia prima*. Now, if the equilibrium of all that arises from a being lies in his heart, that heart is again a rupture of equilibrium, a rupture of equilibrium of the pure Spirit, under the influence of a rupture of *materia prima*.

*

That which loves in man, must love; but it must love something other than what man loves. That which fears in man, must fear; but it must fear something other than what man fears.

For the soul there are two ways to God: love of God and fear of God. Without the one, the soul becomes mean, without the other it becomes foolish.

*

Water extinguishes fire. But water's power over fire can only be relative, because the power of negation over reality can only be relative. For while water can only negate but by no means determine fire, water is always determined by fire.

Man must pray with all that he is; and so too, must he contemplate. Primordial man was nothing other than his prayer, nothing other than a meditation. Thus every prayer should flow back into primordial prayer, unto the mouth

126

of the first man, and every meditation should return to the Divine, through the heart of the first man.

In life the body considers itself infinite, hence it must die; in its dream the soul considers itself infinite, hence it must awaken.

*

Nothing can merely negate; everything must partake of Infinity; therefore the body's pleasure and the soul's plenitude partake of the Spirit through their symbolism. This participation is based upon the vibration that proceeds from the divine, world-creating and world-transforming primordial Breath and is manifested in world ages and human ages, in seasons and the alternation of day and night, resonating for the earthly being in birth and death and breath and blood. The breath is the bridge between body and soul. The body's pleasure should operate in harmony with the vibration which brings about not only the abstinence of the body but also its spiritualisation; the sacred dances of ancient peoples are based upon this knowledge. The breath transmits the vibration realised by the body to the soul. The plenitude of the soul should for its part manifest itself in harmony with the vibration which corresponds to its nature and, along with equanimity, determines the spiritualisation of the soul; the sacred songs of ancient peoples are based upon this knowledge. The vibration realised in the soul is the dance of the soul, as the vibration realised in the body is the song of the body.

Every existence is a rupture of equilibrium. Nothing can exist as mere rupture of equilibrium, neither humanity nor a part of humanity. Therefore every human society must bring its existence into harmony with the Divine, through ritual acts; it must reproduce the original equilibrium in the measure of the given, social, human possibil-

127

ities. If a people no longer has a tradition of this kind, it perishes.

*

The breath is the bridge from the body to the soul; it is also the bridge from multiplicity to unity. Thus it is the bridge from the soul to the Spirit.

Vibration is the knock at the divine Door.

*

The Spirit is pure Act in emptiness.

*

The body suffers from hunger, thirst, wakefulness and chastity. Every abstention purifies, loosens the heavy fabric of error and leads to the Spirit.

*

Water contains, animates; but it can destroy only forcefully and wear down slowly. But fire, on the other hand, does not destroy forcefully, but spiritually. It comes from emptiness and returns to emptiness, it disappears in the ether; it does not mix with what it consumes; it is pure, it comes and goes like a miracle. Water mixes and becomes murky, and what it has worn down devolves upon it. Therefore the action of water corresponds to force, the action of fire to the Spirit.

Thus the Spirit, too, comes from the Divine and returns to the Divine like fire into emptiness.

*

Life is submission, sleep; thus the living man must awaken spiritually and arise. Nothing triumphs without ceaseless, regular repetition; thus water hollows, a saw saws; thus the heartbeat and the breath vanquish ever-threatening death. Thus the spiritual act, the ever-repeated prayer, hollows out the dream, the illusion of life; thus the spiritual act saws, thus it vanquishes life. Without this rhythm and this repetition, without this regular spiritualisation of all necessary actions, man falls prey to suffering.

Illusion must be destroyed, only the Spirit has the right to be; for only the Spirit is.

*

What is the Spirit? Who can say what the Spirit is? Through the Spirit differentiation comes into things; we perceive it where it encounters obstacles. But if there are no obstacles, we do not perceive it; then we are Spirit. With the Spirit it is as with space, which symbolises it; we perceive space by means of the things it differentiates; but if there are no things, we are ourselves space, and we cannot say what space is.

*

Why is the spiritual man not envious of another's happiness? Because apart from his happiness there are only facts, and a fact could not add anything to his happiness.

*

Happiness is a belief. Belief is a happiness. There is no other on earth. Most people want to obtain happiness underhandedly, they want to steal it from the divine Giver, Whom they do not know. In their hands all happiness turns to dust. Who can steal a belief? What can be stolen is not even worth stealing.

*

In every fibre of our being lies the Miracle, undivided and limitless. We are permeated by It and yet distant from It. The Miracle is everything, and in It we are scarcely a grain of sand; but in our error we are the ocean of sand covering the holy Hidden One.

129

*

The Infinite is only real in the Infinite.
The Real is only infinite in the Real.

*

God is both impersonal and personal, and neither one nor the other. He is personal as manifestation in His relations with the individual, that is, with man, because otherwise there would be no point of contact between the human and the divine. But this personal quality appertains to Him no differently than a colour belongs to light made visible by the colour. We are individual, therefore conscious; now insofar as our consciousness signifies no limitation, but rather a spiritual unity, it mirrors the divine Spirit; God answers the utterances of our consciousness, our prayers, but He remains supra-conscious in Himself—not unconscious, not without consciousness, like a stone. Through prayer, which is an indirect effect of God, and in this sense a gift, a grace and a participation in Him, we dissolve the threads of our inner limitations and let the divine light shine through our dark consciousness. Hence God hears our prayers and answers them, without suffering any restriction or alteration in Himself. Now, in Itself the Divine is neither conscious nor unconscious, neither personal nor impersonal; for in the Divine we are contained as pure possibilities and ultimately as primordial Possibility—we have no differentiated existence. One can express the relation between ourselves and God, between effect and Principle, thus: God answers our prayers as if without listening to them; for they do not enter Him, because for Him they are nothing; however the answer proceeds from Him, because He is everything to us—all-hearing, all-knowing; He is the eternal answer and fulfilment. The reflection is touched by the archetype, the effect by the cause—not the reverse. God's answer awaited our prayers before we existed.

*

Man wants to become someone else in every moment in order to escape his finiteness; thus he deludes himself further and believes himself infinite; and symbolically he becomes infinite through every pleasure. Such is life.

The bitterest poverty is still somehow wealth, for one must still possess something in order to be poor. If one were no longer to possess anything, one would no longer exist; pure poverty would be nothingness.

But what is not nothing is everything.

In this sense every man is rich.

*

The content of ignorance is that we do not know what we are. Because we do not know, and to the extent that we do not know, we are men, beings, circles of consciousness. And what we do not know is this: I am nothing except myself.

131

FOURTH COLLECTION

Written *anno* 1932–33 in Mostaghanem*

*Algeria.

WHAT IS PRIMORDIAL MEDITATION? It is the quickening of the intelligence from within, from the Spirit. Just as fire returns to ether when it has nothing more to consume, so, too, the intelligence returns to the Spirit when it has consumed the world and itself. This consuming of the world is primordial meditation. Through it man becomes spiritual man.

In his heart man has an ocean in which he could drown the world, if only he knew it.

In his heart man has a fire with which he could burn the world, if only he knew it.

*

He who is detached from the phenomenal world looks at that world as a unit, a single fact; he who is enmeshed in the world looks at it as multiplicity and answers to this multiplicity, and is divided in it; he is thus like clay flung down, divided and inert. In the inner water, man finds unity and freedom and flows beyond the world's phenomena; in the inner air he rises above them; in the inner fire he consumes them and returns to the inner ether, to the Divine.

To the extent that man is separated from the Divine, he loves multiplicity and looks on the Divine as a mere particularity, as negation of multiplicity; he does not see Infinitude in the Divine, of which multiplicity is only a fragmented reflection.

*

Earth is humanity. Water is Tradition, sacrifice, purification. Air is the Envoy of God, the Word, the Doctrine. Fire is the Holy Spirit, Revelation. Ether is the divine Origin.

*

The smallest thing is a possibility contained within a possibility. Each existent thing is the possibility of a possibility. When a man lifts a finger, a possibility unfolds, which he affirms. If he does not affirm any possibility within a particular domain of possibility, he reaches the centre of that domain, the possibility of all these negated possibilities, until his own possibility is cancelled out by the Spirit. The Spirit is the primordial Possibility, All-Possibility, the Possibility of all possibilities. We are joyless because we live in only one possibility, in the "I" and its domain. We are attached to this one possibility, though its limitations continually cause us suffering; because this, our possibility, symbolises All-Possibility and seemingly contains all possibilities. But All-Possibility is the lost Eden that we are always seeking in our own limited possibility, which translates All-Possibility into a mere sum of co-possibilities. Our possibility is a desert, and our search for Eden is a wandering from one grain of sand to the next. For the desert seems endless; and yet no grain of sand is distinguished from another; the desert is only a single grain of sand.

Beauty is wealth of possibilities; because the Divine is All-Possibility, it can also be called All-Beauty. Ugliness, on the other hand, is a dearth of possibilities.

Only the individual being suffers, not the whole being, the earthly essence. The latter is manifested in all individual beings; it is in joy and proclaims its joy by begetting and sustaining the individual. Unreality takes revenge on the individual, it gives him pain and death.

Man is the expression of that wholeness which is beyond suffering and is in joy, hence his sexual act is pleasure to him; woman is the expression of individuality, hence her sexual act, giving birth, is suffering. But in harmonising with the man's pleasure, the woman,

136

too, experiences pleasure, just as the individual being, afflicted by pain and death, participates in the joy of the whole being, the earthly essence, through all the positive manifestations of his life.

Just as the essence has only joy, man has only joy, sexually; and just as a being has joy and suffering, woman has joy and suffering, sexually.

This is why it is said that God created woman out of the rib of the first human being: because woman, as an expression of the individual being, is a part of the whole being represented by man. Also, in every sexual act man bears innumerable beings, thousands upon thousands, but woman bears only single beings, in most cases just one in each birth. The claim of a man to several women is connected with this idea; if a man desires one woman alone—and it is a question here not just of a particular desire as a fact, but of whether he can in principle find pleasure and sufficiency with one woman—he does not consider the woman as a fragment, but as a prolongation of himself; he considers her in this sense not as Adam's rib, but as Eve. The particular is a mere fragment of the whole; but individuality, or manifestation in the particular, is self-reflection, self-repetition and therefore prolongation for the whole.

Being is prolonged in the same way through existence— not on its own plane and not as pure Being, but on a lower plane and as a reflected self-diminution. Therefore man corresponds to Being, and woman, as exclusive beloved, to existence.

It is true that Being prolongs itself in existence, but not in what exists, in what is present; this is fragmentary, and as fragment it nowhere touches its own existence and Being, removing nothing from them; just as Adam's rib, which became woman, removed nothing from Adam. What exists is always a fragment, because it can never be unique; but existence is unique, and its uniqueness is a reflection of the unity of Being. If Being is man and existence is the exclusively loved woman, then existing things are the many women of the polygamist or the faithless lover.

Man's spirit generalises and breaks asunder; woman's spirit particularises and encloses. Man can create and destroy; woman cannot create and does not destroy; she reproduces and conserves what exists; she lives in facts, as man lives in principles. Man's beauty is his core; woman's spirit is her shell; or, as an Arabic proverb says: man's beauty is in his spirit, and woman's spirit is in her beauty. But in the Spirit we are neither men nor women, but an unfragmented Knowledge.

The concern of childhood is play, so the child must be able to obey. The concern of youth is love, so the youth must be able to overcome. The concern of manhood is fulfilment, so a man must be able to fight. The concern of old age is possession, so the old man must be able to sacrifice.

The spiritual man is truly himself in the Spirit; in his soul he is simultaneously child, youth, adult and old man. He is simple and natural like a child, trusting and ardent like a youth, firm and clear like a man, selfless and mild like an elder.

*

Everything that befalls a man from outside is either an affirmation or a negation; if it is an affirmation, he has no need of it, for his heart is the seal of the primordial divine Affirmation; if it is a negation, it has no need of an answer, for it is only an expression of the original negation, the root of the world, the possibility of contradiction within All-Possibility. And man himself is nothing but negation: thus he can suffer no injustice before God. The ordinary

138

man answers to the innumerable negations that attack him. But were his existence not itself a negation and a kind of transgression, it could never be denied in any way.

*

The Divine is at first glance a determination, and as such It is unconditional Unity. But within Itself this Unity is dissolved in undeterminable Non-Unity, in something Nameless.

*

This is the key to the knowledge of the world: to know that as such, everything that negates, diminishes, fragments has its cause, not in the Divine but rather in the absence of the divine Cause; and that consequently, this absence is to be found included in the divine Possibility—All-Possibility cannot exclude the contradictory possibility of its impossibility. This contradictory possibility lies in All-Possibility like a speck of dust in immeasurable space, and unfolds within itself the whole manifested universe, in which the visible universe is again only a speck of dust. Furthermore this one possibility is itself but the first of all determinations, the primordial determination, that of Unity, of self-determining Being.

*

He who understands Unity and knows he understands it, finds peace. Multiplicity seduces and consumes man; in multiplicity man has countless known and unknown enemies. In Unity he has only one enemy, the illusion of multiplicity, and one Friend, who is stronger than illusion and against which it can do nothing—namely the Spirit.

Beings are crushed because they want to be gods. Every limb suffers only because it would deify itself. There are certainly other ways of expressing the cause of suffering,

139

but ultimately there is no other cause of suffering. Every fibre in a being stands in contradiction to Reality insofar as it appears to be different from Reality and an individual fact; therefore it batters itself sore against Reality, dashes itself against it, it delivers its own judgement; Reality remains untouched. Heaven spits upon him who spits heavenward, with his own spittle. He who could throw a boulder at Heaven, would be crushed by Heaven with the same boulder.

*

He whose imagination is subject to sentiment is bound to a limited horizon; his memory is weak and falsified, his reason obscured. But if his heart is not crippled with regard to the Spirit, and if the Spirit can work on his reason through the heart, then reason undermines sentiment, in which the soul is like a dense, divisible clod of earth. Then man's imagination is free and can move untrammelled like water; but its effectiveness is conditioned by passion and falsifies memory, weakens the intelligence. Now, if man is no longer subject even to his imagination, his memory is no longer determined from below, but from above: it is clear, veracious and sharp. It is restored to health with the emergence of reason and establishes the correct relation of the latter to the ephemeral environment. As fire burns in air, so reason works in the memory. Reason purifies the memory, as sentiment fills the imagination. The spiritual man is inwardly poor, solitary, homeless. He has his joy in himself and is himself the cause of his joys.

*

Everything particular and diverse is as it were sucked out of Reality by nothingness and split and diversified increasingly with distance from Reality, though without being able to approach nothingness, since this does not

140

exist. It is as if things had fallen out of Reality, and were suspended over nothingness; they hang by a hair over the abyss of nothingness. But since this nothingness cannot be, else primordial Affirmation would not be infinite, something that exists must stand in place of the non-existent: a spirit of negation, which wants to set itself up in opposition to Reality, in order to be equal to God through its uniqueness.

*

Man must be born twice, once on earth and once spiritually; therefore he must also die twice, namely in death and in the Spirit. On earth man brings forth first, then he dies; in the Spirit he dies before he brings forth.

*

The heart is ultimately turned away from illusion: its deepest yearning is the Divine. Therefore the heart has a double meaning, because in it there are two aspirations, one outward and one returning; in its depths lies fire, lit from the spiritual ray of the primordial Sun; but it is surrounded by a smoke, a sheath, woven of illusion and the tendency to illusion.

*

Reason attacks, defends, struggles; but the Spirit is pure assertion, pure affirmation of itself.

*

The heart is a twofold centre: as human centre it is the causal root of the "I"; as spiritual centre it is Centre everywhere. Therefore the return to the centre, spiritualisation through contemplation of the participation of all things in the Divine, is a return to the Centre that is everywhere, and a dissolution of the human centre and all its reflections.

141

On the other hand, spiritualisation through the contemplation of the Exclusivity and sole Reality of the Principle is like an entering and solidifying in the present, which was never future and will never be past, but remains always the present.

Salvation through affirmation and through the Centre is salvation through infinitude or perfection.

Salvation through negation and through the present is salvation through Eternity or Reality.

Infinitude is beyond space, because it is everywhere Centre and thus boundless.

Eternity is beyond time, because it is always the present and thus without duration.

The heart as centre of individual human ignorance is here; the Heart as knowing Centre is everywhere.

*

Blood is liquid fire; it connects the body to the soul. Man's soul reposes in his blood, the Spirit dwells in his breath. The breath governs the blood, purifies and transforms it.

*

Primordial man had only the love that reposed in itself, lived from itself, inward-turned and blissful in Unity. Joy and sorrow grew from this love because it turned outward; finally love itself shattered, and hatred arose; from this came anger and fear. Love is positive, constructive; hatred negative, destructive. Joy and anger are active, sorrow and fear passive. Spiritual man is none other than primordial man, realised anew; he has returned to Love that is sovereign and bears its purpose in itself. There is nothing to hate, nothing to attack, nothing to fear; neither is there anything over which man should lament or rejoice. Only he who has reabsorbed everything into Love and has thus realised it in its ultimate Sovereignty, can transcend it. He

142

who would begin by renouncing Love falls under the sway of hatred. The love that is split up into diverse things, is also diminished and fragmented by hatred; he who has renounced hatred and reabsorbed his love into Unity, into the heart, possesses integral, pure Love. This Love is oriented towards the Spirit and consumed in It; it is an aspect of the Spirit itself. Every man loves. There is no other path to the Spirit.

Fragmented love lives from phenomena; it extends its pleasure indefinitely through the imagination; the latter animates love and what results from it—joy and sorrow—just as it also animates hatred, anger and fear. Pure reason—namely, reason determined by the Spirit— dissolves imagination concomitantly with the sentiments. In primordial Love, there is nothing that the soul could imagine; for the beloved is Love itself, and Love, loving itself, becomes Spirit, just as fire, burning itself, becomes ether.

Reason does not live from images, through which it wilfully prolongs phenomena; rather, it receives enough from phenomena to act in the light of their symbolism; it prolongs phenomena not through creative imagination, but through non-creative, merely preserving, memory, which only repeats phenomena.

Originally man saw the diverse in the One, then the One in the diverse. Man must infer the One from the diverse, and to the extent that he grasps the One, know the diverse through the One and dissolve the diverse in Unity.

*

Our thinking is nothing but the fragmented reflection of the limitation and illimitation we have in the heart. There- fore the art of purifying the heart is at the same time the art of thinking purely. In the focal point of the heart is the eye that sees the Divine; but since it sees the Divine integrally, and not as the Divine, it is not different from the Divine, but one with It; it is the Eye of the Divine itself, which sees us in Its undivided Omniscience, and we ourselves are precisely this, Its Sight. The Divine, insofar as it can be called a Knower, has Itself as the object of Its knowledge, and hence is divided into Knower and known only relatively and from our standpoint. But our standpoint is justified in that we are real for ourselves, and the nucleus of our relative reality is precisely the eye of the heart, with which we contemplate the Divine and through which the Divine contemplates Itself and thus us, too, since we are after all included in the Divine and cannot be possible and real outside All-Possibility, outside Reality. The divine Eye contemplates Its manifestation through its innumerable focal points, its hearts, but It contemplates manifestation as such precisely through manifestation—through us. On the other hand the Divine contemplates manifestation not through us but by contemplating Itself, as All-Possibility, All-Reality; in this contemplation, contrary to the contemplation of created things, It is creative as their Principle and therefore manifests the universe. For the creature is passive in this contemplation, it effects nothing and is determined by what it contemplates; but the Divine is on the contrary active in its contemplation: it manifests what it contemplates and determines it, without being determined by it in any way.

Thus man is a tree, grown out of his heart and bearing fruit according to the nature of his heart. But in the centre of the heart is the Eye of the Divine, that enables the tree to grow by seeing Itself, and enables it to die by not seeing it as man. For were It to see the tree as man, It would not see it with the Creator's eye, but would be determined by it. The Divine sees only Reality; were it to see creation as such, It would see unreality and would

144

be determined, fulfilled, by the unreal. As lesser reality It sees us through ourselves; our contemplation is but the fragmented reflection of Its contemplation; therefore our contemplation is still Its contemplation.

*

We participate in the Divine in three ways: firstly, insofar as we are in the world, and through our relation to it; secondly, insofar as we stand before God, and through our relation to Him; thirdly, insofar as we are in the Divine, thus through our relation to Ourselves. In the first sense we are a social being; in the second, an individual being; in the third, the universal Being, the Divine. In the Divine we are unmoved, because we are not different from the Divine; as individuals, insofar as we stand apart from the Divine, our movement is uniform, and this uniformity is translated by the changeless rhythm of forms, through which we serve God; as social beings our movements are many, because the environment and we ourselves are changeable, but this multiplicity of our relationships is again ordered as the outermost transposition and extension of Unity, according to the eternal spiritual determinations.

*

We become free through Knowledge alone; to the extent that we are aware of this, we can no longer become free— even only apparently—through anything else. Knowledge dissolves the knots of ignorance as if from within; if these knots are too tight, they must be loosened violently by the sword of Alexander; this is suffering. In principle we can become fully conscious of the Divine without suffering, in order to see nothing but the Divine, be nothing but the Divine; but we ourselves want suffering, because we want ignorance.

The Spirit does not encumber us: "My yoke is easy and my burden is light."

In the Spirit, Knowledge is Love and Love Knowledge; for Knowledge is nothing but Oneness.

*

Everything about us is the measure of our knowledge.

*

What is the primordial doctrine? It is the knowledge of ultimate relationships, enveloped in forms, manifesting itself in forms, continually returning in fresh shapes throughout human ages and yet remaining eternally the same. This Truth, living in multiple forms, limited by none, always leading back to pure Spirit, is the primordial doctrine.

It is the product of no human thinking. It belongs to no one. He who knows it, possesses it; but in truth, it embraces him and has absorbed the knower into itself— It, the Eternal, has absorbed him who is ephemeral. Thus does the sea absorb a drop. Its entrance is everywhere and nowhere. It is without origin and without end.

Index

harmony, 19, 47, 52, 59, 92, 115, 127
hatred, 71, 115, 142
healing, 116, 140
heart, 58, 73, 75, 84, 88, 105, 107, 116, 126, 135, 138, 141–143; hardened, 106, 113; purifying the, 143; seat of the Intellect, 104; *see also* eye; intellect
Heaven, 114
homage, 47

"I", 15–17, 19–21, 41, 45, 50, 58, 81, 97, 106, 107, 115, 125, 136, 141; and "thou", 80, 81; "I-world", 18
idea, 72, 91
idolatry, 48
ignorance, 15, 18, 33, 43, 52, 54, 68, 88, 93, 99, 101, 107, 111, 114, 121, 131, 145; and knowledge, 40; heart, 142; suffering, 113; *see also* veil
imagination, 25, 26, 105, 140, 143
immersion, 42, 115, 123
Impossibility, 22
individual consciousness, *see* "I"
infinity, 38, 58, 65, 116, 119, 123, 127; and centre, 41; quantitative, 23
injunction, 61
innocence, 38, 59, 90, 92
Intellect, 13, 46, 61, 96; and heart, 104
intellectual power, 27
intelligence, 12, 32, 34, 82, 88, 104, 135, 140
interior side of things, 115

Jesus, 49, 61, 91, 98, 100, 113

joy, 36, 39, 54, 57, 114, 115, 125, 136; and pleasure, 51, 83; beauty, 92; primordial, 52; *see also* pleasure
Judgement Day, 61
justice, 61; divine, 71

king, 121
knower, 9, 111, 144, 146
knowledge, 15, 27, 35, 37, 43, 58, 69, 70, 73, 87, 101, 111, 123, 146; and desire, 89; and grace, 117; and ignorance, 40; and intelligence, 104; and life, 114; and love, 84, 146; and Reality, 73; and will, 14, 55, 56, 71, 89, 95, 107; being touched by Reality, 68; body, 95, 127; breath, 27; divine, 13, 26, 30, 102; effective, 93; equilibrium, 87; factual, 77, 88; freedom, 145; heart, 74, 101, 104; human, 17, 32, 69; impulse, 75; intellect, 61; little, 88; modes, 13; one, 95; our only possession, 83; principial, 93; pure, 18; rational, 76, 97; tree of, 88; true, 87; way of, 96; what we are, 121, 138; wisdom, 63; world as, 21, 103; worldly, 139; *see also* science

language, 27; sacred, 6
Latin nature, 6
law, *see* precepts
learning, 87
liberation, 34, 75, 80, 92, 115; *see also* freedom
life, 78, 83, 124
light, 13, 14, 22, 41, 55, 62, 69, 76, 81, 96, 102, 107; and colour, 130; and darkness, 54;

Divine, 45, 130; men and
women, 59; *see also* fire; rays
love, 26, 38, 60; and doing,
121; and fight, 118; and
hatred, 71; and infinity, 38;
and knowledge, 84; and
sentiment, 96; beauty, 54,
59, 90, 114; fire, 143; fragmented, 143; knowledge,
114, 146; object and subject,
126; of man, 59; of multiplicity, 135; of neighbour, 107;
of phenomena, 45, 92; of
woman, 59, 137; primordial,
59, 142; sacred, 125; sexual,
38; the good, 54; the Spirit,
72; third element, 94
lust, 56, 59

manhood, 138
manifestation, 11, 20, 29, 65,
67, 90, 95, 102, 117, 120,
144; particular, 137
Mary, mother of Jesus, 91, 113
masculine and feminine, 59
materia prima, 95, 103, 125
meditation, 74, 127; primordial, 97
memory, 25, 105, 140, 143
mirror, 64, 89, 124, 130
modernity, 95
mountain, 57
movement, 27, 30, 47, 65, 66,
108, 112
multiplicity, 24, 42, 45, 53, 74,
128, 135, 139; *see also* number
music, 5

negation, 12, 14, 16, 17, 20, 23,
35, 41, 50, 53, 66, 67, 89, 99,
117, 118, 126, 135, 138, 141,
142
non-action, 78

nothingness, 16, 23, 119, 120,
140
nourishment, 112, 121
number, 23, 24, 67, 69, 78, 95,
124, 125; *see also* multiplicity

obedience, 61
ocean, 70, 129, 135
old age, 138
Omphalos, 50
ordinary man, 88, 103, 105,
107, 139

Paradise, 38, 91; *see also* Eden
participation in the Divine, 25,
50, 145
passivity, 15, 44
perception, 19, 89, 104, 114
perfect man, 84
perfection, 49
phenomena, 18, 20, 29, 35, 37,
38, 44, 78, 91, 101, 107, 115,
118, 135; and reason, 143;
and sentiment, 105; centre,
116; decay, 40; desert, 41;
loved, 45, 72, 92; perceived,
13; reaction, 70; reflections,
25; symbolic, 31; traced, 52;
see also creation
pilgrimage, 47
pleasure, 35, 51, 66, 78, 83, 122,
124, 125, 127, 136, 143; *see
also* joy
point, 9, 11, 20, 28, 68, 74, 82,
102, 120, 143
polygamy, 138
possibility, 136, 139
poverty, 18, 93, 131; *see also*
solitude
power, 14, 22, 34, 39, 41, 44,
58, 63, 71, 89, 91, 93, 95, 98,
99, 101, 116; human, 17